The Complete

Slow Cooker

Cookbook UK 2023

1000 Days Effortless and Affordable Recipes for Homemade Slow Cooking Meals with European Measurements & Ingredients and Step By Step Instructions

Matt Wisozk

Table of Contents

Chapter 3 Breads and Sandwiches

Chapter 4 Beef

Chapter 5 Poultry 38

Chapter 6 Pork

Chapter 7 Staples, Sauces, Dips and Dressings

Chapter 8 Snacks and Appetisers

65

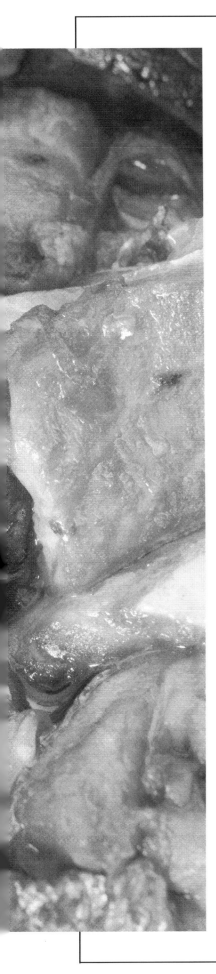

INTRODUCTION

The slow cooker, otherwise known as the Crock-pot is one of the kitchen's favourite countertop appliances. You sure won't find a Slow cooker sitting with dust unused in a kitchen cabinet; they are being used all the time and it's not hard to understand why. They are easy to use and capable of producing the most delicious meals you can think of. You can trust a slow cooker to get the job done, whether it's your favourite lunch or dinner recipes. With this slow cooker, you don't need to stand over the cooker stirring to make sure your meal is cooking; slow cookers generate enough heat to let your food cook properly. Coming home to a hot, slow-cooked meal is a luxury I think we all deserve.

Just as its name goes, it's a cooker that allows foods of all kinds to be cooked at a low and steady temperature over some time. Its "leave-it-and-forget-it" style gives you the freedom to do other things while your delicious meal is cooking in the crock-pot. That just makes your life easier and cooking so much more fun—at least for me. I love to cook, and not just the quick 5-minute chop and fry cooking we do in the morning before rushing off to work. I like to get in there when it comes to my cooking.

The thing that goes into a great meal is not just ingredients and flavours; it's also time. Because of my busy schedule, it's hard for me to cook these meals and try out recipes that take hours to cook well, but that's where the slow cooker has come in and changed my life. I can now cook my favourite chicken recipes in my slow cooker and come home to a nice, slow-cooked chicken with flavour and tenderness. And don't get me started on how this is even a much healthier option than using my regular oven because cooking with my slow cooker means low-fat cooking, saving on energy, and more preserved nutrients than other cooking methods.

What makes the slow cooker even more popular are its recipes. There are so many you can try and just expand your meal palette and give a tasteful twist to your cooking. If your question is, "Where do I find the best and easiest slow cooker recipes?" then you're in absolute culinary luck, because that's what we're offering in this cookbook. You don't have to look any further. This slow cooker cookbook offers a wide variety of recipes with easy-to-get ingredients, easy-to-make steps, and much more. This slow cooker cookbook has become my kitchen companion, and it should be yours too.

Chapter 1 Slow Cooker Basic Guide

The slow cooker is one of the healthiest ways to prepare meals today. You can prepare your favourite meals with a lot less oil than you would normally use when cooking in your regular oven. That means low fat, and that means healthier foods for you. The slow cooker also saves energy. It is way less energy intensive than conventional electric ovens, and that saves you money. So with a slow cooker, you're not just preserving your health; you're also saving money.

Know what else gets preserved with a slow cooker? Nutrients. Because of its cooking style, which involves taking adequate time to slow cook your meals, all those nutrients in your food get locked in and preserved. Like, when you cook meat, for example, all those hours the meat will spend cooking will make the meat more tender and allow all those ingredients and flavours to sift into it much more and give you a more flavourful and tasteful meat. Slow cookers are also really easy to use; you don't have to be a food expert or watch long hours of instructional videos to use one.

There are only a few buttons and components that make it easy to use straight out of the box. There are several types of slow cookers and their different features, but a good slow cooker would come with timer settings to select how long you want the food to cook for and heater settings to control the heat you want the food to cook with.

Features of the Slow Cooker

Cost-Saving Cooking

This is one of the hallmark features of the slow cooker. It costs less to cook with a slow cooker compared to your electric kitchen ovens or even gas cookers. It's been proven that using a conventional electric oven for over an hour can cost around 20 cents, while operating a crock pot for 7 hours costs only 10 cents (that's dependent on your energy consumption); that's a whopping 50% savings on energy. This will make you want to cook more at home, which in turn will help you save money on eating out.

3 Heat Settings

The slow cooker comes with 3 heat settings carefully designed to ensure your meals don't come out overcooked or undercooked. That option gives you control over how you want your meals to be cooked; on a low, high, or keep warm setting. This level of control and options makes cooking with the slow cooker easier and a better alternative to cooking with gas.

Ideal Capacity

The capacity of the slow cooker makes it roomier and makes cooking your favourite meals more convenient. Its 4.7l capacity means it can cook meals for up to 5 people. That's more delicious meals for you, your family, and your friends with just the push of a button. It's perfect for making meals that will serve the whole family.

Dishwasher Safe

You can easily toss the bowl and lid of your slow cooker in the dishwasher without any fear of damage. That just adds to the reasons why the slow cooker is an excellent kitchen appliance. That takes the stress out of washing the bowl and lid of your slow cooker by yourself.

What to Cook in a Slow Cooker

Soups and Stews

Your favourite soups and stews can be prepared in the slow cooker. You'll find some of the best soup recipes in this cookbook that are easy to follow step-by-step and easy to find ingredients as well. When you cook soups in the slow cooker, you are rewarded with richer, more intense flavours in your soup. All you need to do is put all your soup ingredients in the slow cooker, pour the broth on top, and let it work its magic.

Chicken and Seafood

Slow cookers do some of their work with chicken. You won't have chicken that is more tender and flavoured cooked without a slow cooker. In this cookbook, there are insanely good seafood recipes you can try out with your slow cooker. You will get incredibly tasty meals from the slow cooker. Seafood lovers are going to enjoy trying out the different recipes in this slow cooker cookbook that they are going to absolutely love.

Vegetables and Beans

Amazing vegetarian recipes await you in this cookbook for you to try with your slow cooker. Hard root vegetables and dried beans that can cook for hours and still retain their shape and flavour are great to be slow-cooked. Sturdier vegetables like celery, carrots, beets, onions, and potatoes are easier to prepare in a slow cooker.

Beef and Pork

Most beef and pork recipes cook for up to 8 hours to come out tender. Cooking that in your regular oven is going to cost a lot, but with a slow cooker, you don't have to sacrifice your favourite beef recipes. You can slow cook your beef till it's perfectly tenderised and not worry about how much energy you're spending.

Slow Cooker Cooking Tricks

Spray the inside bowl with cooking spray

This will prevent sticking and make cleaning easier. Especially for solid dishes.

Put the harder vegetables at the bottom

Place the harder vegetables that take longer to cook at the bottom where the heat is highest and they can absorb the most moisture to cook better.

Use less liquid

You want to use less liquid when cooking with a slow cooker than you are used to when cooking with your other methods, because meals retain their liquids when cooked in a slow cooker, so you don't end up with too much liquid in your meal.

Omit oil

Since the slow cooker cooks things slowly, your food is not likely to scorch or burn. So you can remove the oil you'll normally add to your recipes when cooking with a slow cooker. This also has the health benefit of reducing your cholesterol intake.

Slow Cooker Cleaning Tips

- Always unplug before cleaning to avoid any electrocution.
- Leave it to clean itself; add a bit of baking soda and dish detergent, fill the bowl with water, and set it on low for 2-4 hours. This is for hard stuck stains and messes.
- White vinegar also does the trick; you can scrub the inner walls of the bowl with a mix of vinegar, baking soda, and detergent to easily remove stains.

Chapter 2 Soups and Stews

Vegetable Beef Soup

Prep time: 15 minutes | Cook time: 4 to 6 hours | Serves 8

450 g extra-lean minced beef
400 g low-salt, stewed tomatoes
300 g low-salt tomato soup
1 onion, chopped
500 ml water
1 (400 g) can chickpeas, drained
2 (200 g) can sweetcorn, drained

400 g sliced canned carrots, drained
225 g diced potatoes
225 g chopped celery
½ teaspoon salt
¼ teaspoon black pepper
Chopped garlic to taste (optional)

1. Sauté minced beef in non-stick skillet or frying pan.
2. Combine all ingredients in slow cooker.
3. Cook on low 4 to 6 hours.

Easy Vegetable Soup

Prep time: 20 minutes | Cook time: 8 to 10 hours | Serves 8 to 10

450 g minced beef, browned
225 g chopped onions
1 (400 g) can kidney beans or butter beans, undrained
225 g sliced carrots
60 g rice, uncooked
950 ml stewed tomatoes

825 ml water
5 beef bouillon or stock cubes
1 tablespoon parsley flakes
1 teaspoon salt
⅛ teaspoon pepper
¼ teaspoon dried basil
1 bay leaf

1. Combine all ingredients in slow cooker.
2. Cover. Cook on low 8 to 10 hours.

Dottie's Creamy Steak Soup

Prep time: 15 minutes | Cook time: 8 to 10 hours | Serves 4 to 6

450 g minced beef
Half a large onion, chopped
340 ml V-8 vegetable juice
2 to 3 medium potatoes, diced
300 g cream of mushroom soup

300 g cream of celery soup
450 g frozen mixed vegetables of your choice
2 teaspoons salt
½ to ¾ teaspoon pepper

1. Sauté beef and onions in skillet or frying pan. Drain.
2. Combine all ingredients in slow cooker.
3. Cover. Cook on low 8 to 10 hours.

Taco Soup with Hominy

Prep time: 15 minutes | Cook time: 4 hours | Serves 8

450 g minced beef
1 envelope dry ranch dressing mix
1 envelope dry taco seasoning mix
1 kg Rotel tomatoes, undrained, alternatively, add salsa to chopped tomatoes

680 g pinto beans, undrained
680 g hominy, undrained - if unavailable, chickpeas, corn, buckwheat grits or polenta meal
1 (400 g) can stewed tomatoes, undrained
1 onion, chopped
500 ml water

1. Brown meat in skillet or frying pan. Pour into slow cooker.
2. Add remaining ingredients. Mix well.
3. Cover. Cook on low 4 hours.

Vegetable Soup with Noodles

Prep time: 15 minutes | Cook time: 2 to 6 hours | Serves 6

565 ml water
2 beef bouillon or stock cubes
1 onion, chopped
450 g minced beef
60 g ketchup
1 teaspoon salt

⅛ teaspoon celery salt
115 g noodles, uncooked
450 g frozen mixed vegetables, or vegetables of your choice
565 ml tomato juice

1. Dissolve bouillon or stock cubes in water.
2. Brown onion and beef in skillet or frying pan. Drain.
3. Combine all ingredients in slow cooker.
4. Cover. Cook on low 6 hours, or on high 2 to 3 hours, until vegetables are tender.

Chilli-Taco Soup

Prep time: 30 minutes | Cook time: 5 to 7 hours | Serves 8

900 g lean stewing meat
2 (400 g) cans stewed tomatoes, Mexican or regular
1 envelope dry taco seasoning

mix
2 (390 g) cans pinto beans
2 (200g) cans sweetcorn
175 ml water

1. Cut large pieces of stewing meat in half and brown in large non-stick skillet or frying pan.
2. Combine all ingredients in slow cooker.
3. Cover and cook on low 5 to 7 hours.

Easy Veggie-Beef Soup

Prep time: 20 minutes | Cook time: 4 to 8 hours |
Serves 6 to 8

450 g browned minced beef, or
450 g stewing steak
450 g sliced carrots
450 g frozen green beans, thawed
400 g sweetcorn, drained, or
450 g frozen corn, thawed
2 (400 g) cans chopped tomatoes

750 ml beef or vegetable broth or stock
3 teaspoons instant beef bouillon or stock
2 teaspoons Worcestershire sauce
1 tablespoon sugar
1 tablespoon minced onion
300 g cream of celery soup

1. Place meat in bottom of slow cooker.
2. Add remaining ingredients except celery soup. Mix well.
3. Stir in soup.
4. Cover. Cook on low 7 to 8 hours, or on high 4 hours.
5. If using stewing meat, shred and mix through soup just before serving.
6. Serve.

Hamburger Vegetable Soup

Prep time: 20 minutes | Cook time: 8 to 9 hours |
Serves 8 to 10

450 g ground braising steak
1 onion, chopped
2 garlic cloves, minced
1 litre V-8 juice
1 (400 g) can stewed tomatoes
450 g coleslaw mix
450 g frozen green beans

450 g frozen sweetcorn
2 tablespoons Worcestershire sauce
1 teaspoon dried basil
½ teaspoon salt
¼ teaspoon pepper

1. Brown beef, onion, and garlic in skillet or frying pan. Drain and transfer to slow cooker.
2. Add remaining ingredients to slow cooker and combine.
3. Cover. Cook on low 8 to 9 hours.

Zesty Taco Soup

Prep time: 15 minutes | Cook time: 4 to 6 hours |
Serves 6 to 8

450 g minced beef
1 large onion, chopped
450 g Mexican-style or underripe tomatoes
450 g ranch-style or pinto beans
450 g sweetcorn, undrained

450 g kidney beans, undrained
450 g black beans, undrained
450 g picante sauce
Corn or tortilla chips
Sour cream
Shredded Cheddar cheese

1. Brown meat and onions in skillet or frying pan. Drain.
2. Combine with all other vegetables and picante sauce in slow cooker.
3. Cover. Cook on low 4 to 6 hours.
4. Serve with corn or tortilla chips, sour cream, and shredded cheese as toppings.

Taco Soup with Pizza Sauce

Prep time: 15 minutes | Cook time: 3 to 4 hours |
Serves 8 to 10

900 g minced beef, browned
1 small onion, chopped and sautéed in minced beef drippings
¾ teaspoon salt
½ teaspoon pepper

1½ packages dry taco seasoning
950 ml pizza sauce
950 ml water
Tortilla chips
Shredded Mozzarella cheese
Sour cream

1. Combine minced beef, onion, salt, pepper, taco seasoning, pizza sauce, and water in 4.5 litre, or larger, slow cooker.
2. Cover. Cook on low 3 to 4 hours.
3. Top individual servings with tortilla chips, cheese, and sour cream.

Taco Soup Plus

Prep time: 15 minutes | Cook time: 6 to 8 hours |
Serves 6

Soup:
450 g extra-lean minced beef or minced turkey
1 medium onion, chopped
1 medium green pepper, chopped
1 envelope dry reduced-salt taco seasoning
125 ml water
1 litre reduced-salt vegetable juice
225 g chunky salsa

Toppings:
175 g shredded lettuce
6 tablespoons fresh tomato, chopped
6 tablespoons low-fat Cheddar cheese, shredded
60 g spring onions or chives, chopped
60 ml fat-free sour cream or fat-free plain yoghurt
Baked tortilla or corn chips

1. Brown meat with onion in non-stick skillet or frying pan. Drain.
2. Combine all soup ingredients in slow cooker.
3. Cover. Cook on low 6 to 8 hours.
4. Serve with your choice of toppings.

Pizza in a Bowl

Prep time: 10 minutes | Cook time: 5 to 6 hours |
Serves 6

740 g fat-free, low-salt marinara sauce
1 (400 g) can low-salt chopped tomatoes
115 g low-fat pepperoni, diced or sliced
340 g fresh mushrooms, sliced

1 large pepper, diced
1 large red onion, chopped
250 ml water
1 tablespoon Italian seasoning
225 g dry macaroni
Low-fat shredded Mozzarella cheese

1. Combine all ingredients, except cheese, in cooker.
2. Cover. Cook on low 5 to 6 hours.
3. Ladle into soup bowls. Sprinkle with cheese.

Steak Soup

Prep time: 20 minutes | Cook time: 4 to 12 hours |
Serves 10 to 12

900 g coarsely minced braising
steak, browned and drained
1.25 litres water
1 large onion, chopped
4 ribs celery, chopped
3 carrots, sliced
2 (400 g) cans chopped
tomatoes

280 g frozen mixed vegetables
5 tablespoons beef-based stock
or gravy granules, or 5 beef
bouillon or stock cubes
½ teaspoon pepper
115 g butter, melted
115 g flour
2 teaspoons salt

1.Combine steak, water, onion, celery, carrots, tomatoes, mixed
vegetables, beef granules, and pepper in slow cooker.
2.Cover. Cook on low 8 to 12 hours, or on high 4 to 6 hours.
3.One hour before serving, turn to high. Make a paste of melted
butter and flour. Stir until smooth. Pour into slow cooker and stir
until well blended. Add salt.
4.Cover. Continue cooking on high until thickened.

Hearty Lentil and Sausage Stew

Prep time: 10 minutes | Cook time: 4 to 6 hours |
Serves 6

225 g dry lentils, picked over and rinsed
1 (400 g) can chopped tomatoes
2 litres chicken broth or stock/stock or water
1 tablespoon salt
225 to 450 g pork or beef sausages, cut into 2-inch pieces

1.Place lentils, tomatoes, chicken broth or stock, and salt in slow
cooker. Stir to combine. Place sausage pieces on top.
2.Cover and cook on low 4 to 6 hours, or until lentils are tender but
not dry or mushy.

Everyone's Hungry Soup

Prep time: 45 minutes | Cook time: 8 to 10 hours |
Serves 20 to 25

6 thick slices bacon
1.4 kg boneless stewing steak,
cubed
450 g boneless pork, cubed
3 (400 g cans tomatoes
285 g Rotel tomatoes and
chillies, alternatively add salsa
to chopped tomatoes
3 celery ribs, chopped
3 large onions, chopped
Garlic to taste
Salt to taste
Pepper to taste

125 ml Worcestershire sauce
2 tablespoons chilli powder
500 ml water
6 to 8 medium potatoes, peeled
and cubed
450 g carrots, sliced
425 g canned English peas,
undrained
1 (400 g) can green beans,
undrained
2 (200 g) cans sweetcorn,
undrained
450 g cut-up okra (optional)

1.Fry bacon in skillet or frying pan until crisp. Remove bacon, but
reserve drippings. Crumble bacon and divide between 2 large (5.7

litre or larger) slow cookers.
2.Brown stewing steak and pork in skillet or frying pan in bacon
drippings.
3.Combine all ingredients and divide between slow cookers.
4.Cover. Cook on low 8 to 10 hours.
5.Serve.

Hamburger-Sausage Soup

Prep time: 25 minutes | Cook time: 8 to 10 hours |
Serves 4 to 6

450 g minced beef
450 g Polish sausage, sliced
½ teaspoon seasoned salt
¼ teaspoon dried oregano
¼ teaspoon dried basil
1 package dry onion soup mix
(or combine onion powder with
mixed herbs)

1.5 litres boiling water
1 (400 g) can chopped tomatoes
1 tablespoon soy sauce
115 g sliced celery
115 g chopped celery leaves
225 g pared, sliced carrots
225 g macaroni, uncooked

1.Brown minced beef and sausage in skillet or frying pan. Drain.
Place in slow cooker.
2.Add seasoned salt, oregano, basil, and onion soup mix to cooker.
3.Stir in boiling water, tomatoes, and soy sauce.
4.Add celery, celery leaves, and carrots. Stir well.
5.Cover. Cook on low 8 to 10 hours.
6.One hour before end of cooking time, stir in dry macaroni.
7.Serve.

Overnight Bean Soup

Prep time: 10 minutes | Cook time: 5¼ to 11¼ hours
| Serves 6 to 8

450 g dry small white beans e.g.
haricot beans
1.5 litres water
500 ml boiling water
2 large carrots, diced
3 ribs celery, diced
2 teaspoons chicken stock
granules, or 2 chicken stock
cubes
1 bay leaf

½ teaspoon dried thyme
½ teaspoon salt
¼ teaspoon pepper
60 g chopped fresh parsley
1 envelope dry onion soup mix
(or combine onion powder with
mixed herbs)
Crispy, crumbled bacon
(optional)

1.Rinse beans. Combine beans and 1.5 litres water in saucepan.
Bring to boil. Reduce heat to low and simmer 2 minutes. Remove
from heat. Cover and let stand 1 hour or overnight.
2.Place beans and soaking water in slow cooker.
3.Add 500 ml boiling water, carrots, celery, bouillon/stock, bay
leaf, thyme, salt, and pepper. Cover. Cook on high 5 to 5½ hours, or
on low 10 to 11 hours, until beans are tender.
4.Stir in parsley and soup mix. Cover. Cook on high 10 to 15
minutes.
5.Remove bay leaf. Garnish individual servings with bacon.

Delicious Sausage Soup

Prep time: 15 minutes | Cook time: 4 to 5 hours |
Serves 4

1.4 litres chicken stock
115 ml double cream
3 carrots, grated
4 potatoes, sliced or cubed
900 g kale, chopped

450 g spicy Italian sausage,
browned
½ teaspoon salt
½ teaspoon crushed red pepper
flakes

1. Combine broth or stock and cream in slow cooker. Turn on high.
2. Add carrots, potatoes, kale, and sausage.
3. Sprinkle spices over top.
4. Cover. Cook on high 4 to 5 hours, stirring occasionally.

Spicy Sausage Soup

Prep time: 25 minutes | Cook time: 6 to 8 hours |
Serves 8 to 10

450 g minced beef
450 g spicy sausage (casings
removed)
Half a large onion, chopped
225 g chopped carrots
225 g chopped celery
1 green or red pepper, chopped
(optional)
2 teaspoons salt, or to taste
¼ teaspoon pepper, or to taste

1 teaspoon dried oregano, or to
taste
2 or 3 garlic cloves, minced
1 (390 g) can stewed or
chopped tomatoes with chillies
1 (400 g) can green beans
¼ teaspoon chilli powder
225 g instant (microwaveable)
rice, uncooked

1. Combine beef, sausage, and onions. Form into balls. Place in slow cooker.
2. Add all remaining ingredients, except rice. Stir gently so as not to break up the meatballs.
3. Cover. Cook on low 6 to 8 hours. Stir in rice 20 minutes before serving.
4. Serve.

Toscano Soup

Prep time: 20 minutes | Cook time: 6 to 8 hours |
Serves 4 to 6

2 medium russet or Maris Piper
potatoes
450 g spicy Italian sausage
1.4 litres chicken stock or low-
salt chicken broth or stock

450 g chopped kale
½ teaspoon crushed red pepper
flakes (optional)
125 ml cream or evaporated
milk

1. Cut potatoes into ½-inch cubes. Place in slow cooker.
2. Grill, broil, or brown sausage in a non-stick skillet or frying pan. When cool enough to handle, cut into ½-inch-thick slices.
3. Add sliced sausage to slow cooker. Stir in all remaining ingredients, except cream.
4. Cover and cook on low 6 to 8 hours.
5. Fifteen to 20 minutes before serving, add cream or evaporated milk and cook until soup is heated through.

Taco Bean Soup

Prep time: 10 minutes | Cook time: 1½ hours |
Serves 12

340 g lean pork sausages
450 g extra-lean minced beef
1 envelope dry low-salt taco
seasoning
1 litre water
2 (400 g) cans kidney beans,
rinsed and drained

2 (400 g) cans low-salt stewed/
chopped tomatoes
800 g diced Mexican tomatoes
with juice or use underripe
tomatoes
1 (450 g) jar chunky salsa

1. Cook sausage and beef in a non-stick skillet or frying pan over medium heat until no longer pink. Spoon into slow cooker.
2. Add taco seasoning and mix well.
3. Stir in water, beans, tomatoes, and salsa.
4. Cover. Cook on high 1 hour.
5. Uncover. Cook another 30 minutes. Stir occasionally. Serve.

Bean and Ham Soup

Prep time: 30 minutes | Cook time: 9 to 11 hours |
Serves 10

450 g mixed dry beans
Ham bone from half a ham
shank
350 g ham, cubed
1 large chopped onion
175 g chopped celery
175 g sliced or chopped carrots
1 (400 g) can low-salt diced/
chopped tomatoes
2 tablespoons chopped parsley

250 ml low-salt tomato juice
1.25 litres water
2 tablespoons Worcestershire
sauce
1 bay leaf
1 teaspoon prepared mustard
½ teaspoon chilli powder
Juice of 1 lemon
1 teaspoon salt
½ teaspoon black pepper

1. Place beans in saucepan. Cover with water and soak overnight. Drain.
2. Cover beans with fresh water and cook in saucepan 30 minutes uncovered. Drain again. Discard water.
3. Combine beans with remaining ingredients in slow cooker.
4. Cover. Cook on low 9 to 11 hours.
5. Remove bay leaf and ham bone before serving.

Chet's Trucker Stew

Prep time: 15 minutes | Cook time: 2 to 3 hours |
Serves 8

450 g pork sausages, cooked
and drained
450 g minced beef, cooked and
drained
2 (395 g) cans pork and beans,
or beans and pork sausages
1 (400 g) can light kidney beans

1 (400 g) can dark kidney beans
2 (400 g) cans butter beans,
drained
225 g ketchup
225 g brown sugar
1 tablespoon spicy prepared
mustard

1. Combine all ingredients in slow cooker.
2. Cover. Simmer on high 2 to 3 hours.

Hearty Bean and Vegetable Soup

Prep time: 25 minutes | Cook time: 6 to 8 hours |
Serves 6 to 8

2 medium onions, sliced
2 garlic cloves, minced
2 tablespoons olive oil
2 litres chicken or vegetable
broth or stock
1 small head cabbage, chopped
2 large red potatoes, chopped
450 g chopped celery

450 g chopped carrots
450 g sweetcorn
2 teaspoons dried basil
1 teaspoon dried marjoram
¼ teaspoon dried oregano
1 teaspoon salt
½ teaspoon pepper
2 (400 g) cans haricot beans

1. Sauté onions and garlic in oil. Transfer to large slow cooker.
2. Add remaining ingredients, mixing together well.
3. Cover. Cook on low 6 to 8 hours.

Taco Twist Soup

Prep time: 10 minutes | Cook time: 4 to 6 hours |
Serves 6 to 8

1 medium onion, chopped
2 garlic cloves, minced
2 tablespoons rapeseed or olive
oil
675 g reduced-salt beef or
vegetable broth or stock
1 (400 g) can black beans,
rinsed and drained
1 (400 g) can chopped

tomatoes, undrained
375 ml picante sauce
225 g spiral pasta (fusilli or
rotini), uncooked
1 small green pepper, chopped
2 teaspoons chilli powder
1 teaspoon ground cumin
115 g shredded low-fat cheese
Fat-free sour cream (optional)

1. Sauté onions and garlic in oil in skillet or frying pan.
2. Combine all ingredients except cheese and sour cream.
3. Cook on low 4 to 6 hours, or just until pasta is tender.
4. Add cheese and sour cream as desired when serving.

White Bean and Barley Soup

Prep time: 15 minutes | Cook time: 8 to 10 hours |
Serves 12

1 large onion, chopped
2 garlic cloves, minced
1 tablespoon olive or rapeseed
oil
1.3 kg butter beans, undrained
1 litre fat-free, low-salt chicken
broth or stock
1 litre water
2 large carrots, chopped
2 medium green or red peppers,

chopped
2 celery ribs, chopped
115 g quick-cooking barley
60 g chopped fresh parsley
2 bay leaves
½ teaspoon dried thyme
¼ teaspoon black pepper
2 (400 g) cans chopped
tomatoes, undrained

1. Sauté onion and garlic in oil in skillet or frying pan until just wilted.
2. Combine all ingredients in slow cooker.
3. Cook on low 8 to 10 hours.
4. Discard bay leaves before serving.

French Market Soup

Prep time: 10 minutes | Cook time: 10 hours |
Serves 8

450 g dry bean or four bean
mix, washed with stones
removed
1.9 litres water
1 ham hock
1 teaspoon salt
¼ teaspoon pepper

1 (400 g) can tomatoes
1 large onion, chopped
1 garlic clove, minced
1 chilli pepper, chopped, or 1
teaspoon chilli powder
60 ml lemon juice

1. Combine all ingredients in slow cooker.
2. Cover. Cook on low 8 hours. Turn to high and cook an additional 2 hours, or until beans are tender.
3. Debone ham, cut meat into bite-sized pieces, and stir back into soup.

Bean and Bacon Soup

Prep time: 25 minutes | Cook time: 11 to 13½ hours |
Serves 6

285 g dried bean soup mix, or
any combination of mixed dried
beans
1.25 litres water
1 onion, chopped
750 ml water

4 slices fried bacon (precooked
bacon works well), crumbled
1 envelope taco seasoning
2 (400 g) cans chopped
tomatoes, undrained

1. Place dried beans in large stockpot. Cover with 1.25 litres water. Cover pot and bring to a boil. Cook 2 minutes over high heat.
2. Remove pot from heat and allow to stand, covered, for 1 hour. Return pot to the hob and cook covered for 2½ to 3 hours, or until beans are tender. Drain.
3. Combine cooked beans, onion, 750 ml water, bacon, and taco seasoning in slow cooker. Mix well.
4. Cook on low 8 to 10 hours.
5. Add tomatoes. Stir well. Cook another 30 minutes.

Minced beef Vegetable Soup

Prep time: 15 minutes | Cook time: 8 to 9 hours |
Serves 10

450 g minced beef
1.3 kg tomato or V-8, juice
450 g frozen mixed vegetables,
thawed
450 g frozen cubed hash

browns, thawed
1 envelope dry onion soup mix
(or combine onion powder with
mixed herbs)

1. Brown beef in non-stick skillet or frying pan on the hob. Drain.
2. Place beef in slow cooker. Stir in remaining ingredients.
3. Cover and cook on low 8 to 9 hours, or until vegetables are cooked through.

Hamburger-Lentil Soup

Prep time: 20 minutes | Cook time: 4 to 10 hours |
Serves 8

450 g minced beef	1 tablespoon salt
115 g chopped onions	450 g dry lentils, washed with
4 carrots, diced	stones removed
3 ribs celery, diced	950 ml water
1 garlic clove, minced, or 1	½ teaspoon dried marjoram
teaspoon garlic powder	1 tablespoon brown sugar
950 ml tomato juice	

1. Brown minced beef and onion in skillet or frying pan. Drain.
2. Combine all ingredients in slow cooker.
3. Cover. Cook on low 8 to 10 hours, or on high 4 to 6 hours.

Bean and Herb Soup

Prep time: 45 minutes | Cook time: 1 hour | Serves 6
to 8

350 g dry mixed beans	1 to 2 teaspoons fresh basil, or
1.25 litres water	½ teaspoon dried basil
1 ham hock	1 to 2 teaspoons fresh oregano,
2252 g chopped onions	or ½ teaspoon dried oregano
225 g chopped celery	1 to 2 teaspoons fresh thyme, or
225 g chopped carrots	½ teaspoon dried thyme
500 to 750 ml water	450 g fresh tomatoes, crushed,
1 teaspoon salt	or 1 (400 g) can crushed/
¼ to ½ teaspoon pepper	chopped tomatoes

1. Combine beans, water, and ham in saucepan. Bring to boil. Turn off heat and let stand 1 hour.
2. Combine onions, celery, and carrots in the water in another saucepan. Cook until soft. Mash slightly.
3. Combine all ingredients in slow cooker.
4. Cover. Cook on high 2 hours, and then on low 2 hours.

Black Bean and Ham Soup

Prep time: 20 minutes | Cook time: 7½ to 10 hours |
Serves 18

900 g dry black beans or black turtle beans	¼ to ½ teaspoon pepper
4.75 litres water	3 cloves minced garlic
Ham bone, ham pieces, or ham hocks	4 celery ribs, chopped
	3 large onions, chopped
3 bunches of spring onions, thinly sliced	300 g consommé
	115 g butter
4 bay leaves	2½ tablespoons flour
1 tablespoon salt	250 ml Madeira wine (optional)
	Chopped parsley

1. In 5.7-litre slow cooker, soak beans in water for 8 hours. Rinse. Drain. Pour beans back into slow cooker or divide between 2 (3.8 to 5.7-litre) cookers.
2. Add ham, spring onions, bay, salt, pepper, garlic, celery, and onions. Pour in consommé. Add water to cover vegetables and meat.

3. Cover. Cook on high 1½ to 2 hours. Reduce heat to low and cook for 6 to 8 hours.
4. Remove ham bones and bay leaves. Cut ham off bones and set meat aside.
5. Force vegetable mixture through sieve, if you wish.
6. Taste and adjust seasonings, adding more salt and pepper if needed. Return cooked ingredients and cut-up ham to cooker.
7. In saucepan, melt 115g butter. Stir in flour until smooth. Stir into soup to thicken and enrich.
8. Prior to serving, add wine to heated soup mixture. Garnish with chopped parsley.

Northern Bean Soup

Prep time: 15 minutes | Cook time: 12 to 14 hours |
Serves 6 to 8

450 g dry Northern beans or butter beans	tomatoes
	4 carrots, peeled and chopped
450 g ham	115 g green chilli peppers
2 medium onions, chopped	1 teaspoon garlic powder
Half a green pepper, chopped	950 ml to 1.9 litres water
225 g chopped celery	2 to 3 teaspoons salt
1 (400 g) can diced/chopped	

1. Wash beans. Cover with water and soak overnight. Drain. Pour into slow cooker.
2. Dice ham into 1-inch pieces. Add to beans.
3. Stir in remaining ingredients.
4. Cover. Cook on high 2 hours, then on low 10 to 12 hours, or until beans are tender.

Caribbean-Style Black Bean Soup

Prep time: 10 minutes | Cook time: 4 to 10 hours |
Serves 8 to 10

450 g dried black beans, washed and stones removed	2 teaspoons dried oregano
	1 teaspoon dried thyme
3 onions, chopped	1 tablespoon salt
1 green pepper, chopped	½ teaspoon pepper
4 cloves garlic, minced	750 ml water
1 ham hock, or 175 g cubed ham	2 tablespoons vinegar
	Sour cream
1 tablespoon oil	Fresh chopped coriander
1 tablespoon ground cumin	

1. Soak beans overnight in 3.8 litres water. Drain.
2. Combine beans, onions, green pepper, garlic, ham, oil, cumin, oregano, thyme, salt, pepper, and 750 ml fresh water. Stir well.
3. Cover. Cook on low 8 to 10 hours, or on high 4 to 5 hours.
4. For a thick soup, remove half of cooked bean mixture and purée until smooth in blender or mash with potato masher. Return to cooker. If you like a thinner soup, leave as is.
5. Add vinegar and stir well. Debone ham, cut into bite-sized pieces, and return to soup.
6. Serve in soup bowls with a dollop of sour cream in the middle of each individual serving, topped with fresh coriander.

Vegetarian Chilli Soup

Prep time: 10 minutes | Cook time: 4 to 9½ hours |
Serves 8

1 large onion, chopped	stewed or chopped tomatoes
1 tablespoon margarine	1.25 litres water
1 clove garlic, finely chopped	½ teaspoon salt
2 teaspoons chilli powder	¼ teaspoon black pepper
½ teaspoon dried oregano, crumbled	340 g fresh kale
800 ml vegetable broth or stock	75 g white long grain rice
1 (400 g) can no-added-salt	540 g cannellini beans, drained and rinsed

1. Sauté onion in skillet or frying pan with margarine until tender.
2. Add garlic, chilli powder, and oregano. Cook for 30 seconds. Pour into slow cooker.
3. Add remaining ingredients except kale, rice, and beans.
4. Cover. Cook on low 7 hours, or on high 3 to 4 hours.
5. Cut kale stalks into small pieces and chop leaves coarsely.
6. Add to soup with rice and beans.
7. Cover. Cook on high 1 to 2½ hours more, or until rice is tender and kale is done to your liking.

Minced beef Bean Soup

Prep time: 25 minutes | Cook time: 3 to 4 hours |
Serves 8

900 g minced beef	300 g Cheddar cheese soup or
3 (400 g) cans pinto beans, drained	soup with cheese such as leek and cheddar
600 g tomato soup	Salt and pepper to taste

1. Brown beef in large non-stick skillet or frying pan. Drain.
2. Place browned beef in slow cooker. Add remaining ingredients and mix well.
3. Cover and cook on low 3 to 4 hours, or until soup is hot and until flavours have blended.

Chicken Tortilla Soup

Prep time: 10 minutes | Cook time: 8 hours | Serves
6 to 8

4 chicken breast halves	225 g salsa, your choice of heat
2 (400 g) cans black beans, undrained	115 g chopped green chillies
800 g Mexican stewed tomatoes, or Rotel tomatoes, or add salsa to chopped tomatoes	400 g tomato sauce
	Tortilla chips
	450 g shredded cheese

1. Combine all ingredients except chips and cheese in large slow cooker.
2. Cover. Cook on low 8 hours.
3. Just before serving, remove chicken breasts and slice into bite-sized pieces. Stir into soup.
4. To serve, put a handful of chips in each individual soup bowl. Ladle soup over chips. Top with cheese.

Sauerkraut-Sausage Bean Soup

Prep time: 10 minutes | Cook time: 2 to 3 hours |
Serves 8 to 10

3 (400 g) cans white beans, undrained	450 g sausages, sliced
450 g sauerkraut, drained and rinsed	60 g brown sugar
	115 g ketchup

1. Combine all ingredients in slow cooker.
2. Cover. Cook on high 2 to 3 hours.
3. Serve.

Beef 'n Black Bean Soup

Prep time: 30 minutes | Cook time: 5 to 7 hours |
Serves 10

450 g extra-lean minced beef	1 tablespoon sugar
800 ml fat-free, low-salt chicken broth or stock	1½ teaspoons dried basil
1 (400 g) can low-salt, chopped tomatoes, undrained	½ teaspoon salt
8 spring onions, thinly sliced	½ teaspoon dried oregano
3 medium carrots, thinly sliced	½ teaspoon ground cumin
2 celery ribs, thinly sliced	½ teaspoon chilli powder
2 garlic cloves, minced	2 (400 g) cans black beans, rinsed and drained
	350 g rice, cooked

1. In a non-stick skillet or frying pan over medium heat, cook beef until no longer pink. Drain.
2. Place beef in slow cooker.
3. Add remaining ingredients except black beans and rice.
4. Cover. Cook on high 1 hour.
5. Reduce to low. Cook 4 to 5 hours, or until vegetables are tender.
6. Add beans and rice.
7. Cook 1 hour longer on low, or until heated through.

Mexican Rice and Bean Soup

Prep time: 15 minutes | Cook time: 6 hours | Serves 6

115 g chopped onions	undrained
75 g chopped green peppers	375 ml water
1 garlic clove, minced	115 g long grain rice, uncooked
1 tablespoon oil	1 teaspoon paprika
115 g package sliced or chopped dried beef	½ to 1 teaspoon chilli powder
500 ml tomato juice	½ teaspoon salt
1 (400 g) can red kidney beans,	Dash of pepper

1. Cook onions, green peppers, and garlic in oil in skillet or frying pan until vegetables are tender but not brown. Transfer to slow cooker.
2. Tear beef into small pieces and add to slow cooker.
3. Add remaining ingredients. Mix well.
4. Cover. Cook on low 6 hours. Stir before serving.
5. Serve.

Garbanzo Souper

Prep time: 20 minutes | Cook time: 6 hours | Serves 6

450 g dry chickpeas
113 g raw baby carrots, cut in halves
1 large onion, diced
3 ribs celery, cut in 1-inch pieces
1 large green pepper, diced
½ teaspoon dried basil
½ teaspoon dried oregano

½ teaspoon dried rosemary
½ teaspoon dried thyme
1.6 litres vegetable broth or stock
1 broth or stock can of water
225g tomato sauce
250 g prepared hummus
½ teaspoon sea salt

1. Soak beans overnight. Drain. Place in bottom of slow cooker.
2. Add carrots, onion, celery, and green pepper.
3. Sprinkle with basil, oregano, rosemary, and thyme.
4. Cover with broth or stock and water.
5. Cover. Cook on high 6 hours.
6. Half an hour before serving, stir in tomato sauce, hummus, and salt. Cook until hot.
7. Serve.

Bean Soup

Prep time: 10 minutes | Cook time: 5½ to 13 hours | Serves 10 to 12

225 g dry butter beans
225 g dry red beans or pinto beans
1 litre water
2 (400 g) cans chopped tomatoes
1 medium onion, chopped
2 tablespoons vegetable

bouillon granules, or 4 bouillon or stock cubes
2 garlic cloves, minced
2 teaspoons Italian seasoning, crushed
255 g frozen green beans, thawed

1. Soak and rinse dried beans.
2. Combine all ingredients except green beans in slow cooker.
3. Cover. Cook on high 5½ to 6½ hours, or on low 11 to 13 hours.
4. Stir green beans into soup during last 2 hours.

Black Bean and Tomato Soup

Prep time: 15 minutes | Cook time: 8 hours | Serves 6

450 g black beans
560 g Rotel tomatoes or add salsa to chopped tomatoes
1 medium onion, chopped
1 medium green pepper, chopped

1 tablespoon minced garlic
400 g chicken or vegetable broth or stock
Water
Cajun seasoning to taste

1. Cover beans with water and soak for 8 hours or overnight. Drain well. Place beans in slow cooker.
2. Add tomatoes, onions, pepper, garlic, and chicken or vegetable broth or stock. Add water just to cover beans. Add Cajun seasoning.
3. Cover. Cook on high 8 hours. Mash some of the beans before serving for a thicker consistency.
4. Serve.

Pinto Beans and Ham Soup

Prep time: 10 minutes | Cook time: 10 hours | Serves 10

450 g dried pinto beans
1.4 litres water
115 g cooked ham, chopped
1 clove garlic, minced
1 tablespoon chilli powder

1 teaspoon salt
1 teaspoon black pepper
¼ teaspoon dried oregano
¼ teaspoon ground cumin

1. Cover beans with water and soak overnight, or 6 to 8 hours.
2. In the morning, drain and rinse beans, discard soaking water, and put beans in slow cooker.
3. Add remaining ingredients, including 1.4 litres fresh water.
4. Cover. Cook on low 10 hours.
5. Stir once or twice if possible, during cooking time.

Mexican Black Bean Soup

Prep time: 10 minutes | Cook time: 6 to 8 hours | Serves 8

800 ml fat-free low-salt chicken broth or stock
225 g chopped onions
2 teaspoons minced garlic
675 g fat-free black beans
2 teaspoons chilli powder
¾ teaspoon ground cumin

800 g Mexican tomatoes with green chillies or jalapeños, alternatively use underripe tomatoes
¾ teaspoon lemon juice
1 bunch spring onions
Fat-free sour cream

1. Combine all ingredients except spring onions and sour cream in slow cooker.
2. Cover. Cook on low 6 to 8 hours.
3. Top each individual serving with sliced spring onions sprinkled over a spoonful of sour cream.

Navy Bean and Bacon Chowder

Prep time: 15 minutes | Cook time: 7¼ to 9¼ hours | Serves 6

350 g dried haricot beans or haricot beans
500 ml cold water
8 slices bacon, cooked and crumbled
2 medium carrots, sliced
1 rib celery, sliced

1 medium onion, chopped
1 teaspoon dried Italian seasoning
⅛ teaspoon pepper
1.3 ml can chicken broth or stock
250 ml milk

1. Soak beans in 500 ml cold water for 8 hours or overnight.
2. After beans have soaked, drain, if necessary, and place in slow cooker.
3. Add all remaining ingredients, except milk, to slow cooker.
4. Cover. Cook on low 7 to 9 hours, or until beans are crisp-tender.
5. Place 450 g cooked bean mixture into blender. Process until smooth. Return to slow cooker.
6. Add milk. Cover and heat on high 10 minutes.
7. Serve for diners.

White Bean Fennel Soup

Prep time: 15 minutes | Cook time: 1 to 3 hours |
Serves 6

1 tablespoon olive or rapeseed oil	cannellini beans, rinsed and drained
1 large onion, chopped	1 (400 g) can chopped tomatoes, undrained
1 small fennel bulb, thinly sliced	1 teaspoon dried thyme
1.25 litres fat-free chicken broth or stock	¼ teaspoon black pepper
	1 bay leaf
1 (400 g) can white kidney or	680 g chopped fresh spinach

1. Sauté onions and fennel in oil in skillet or frying pan until brown.
2. Combine onions, fennel, broth or stock/stock, beans, tomatoes, thyme, pepper, and bay leaf.
3. Cook on low for several hours, or on high for 1 hour, until fennel and onions are tender.
4. Remove bay leaf.
5. Add spinach about 10 minutes before serving.

Hearty Bean Soup

Prep time: 30 minutes | Cook time: 4 to 5 hours |
Serves 6

3 (390 g) cans pinto beans, undrained	1 green pepper, chopped
3 (400 g) cans butter beans, undrained	1 sweet red pepper, chopped (optional)
1 litre chicken or vegetable broth or stock	2 garlic cloves, minced
3 potatoes, peeled and chopped	1 teaspoon salt, or to taste
4 carrots, sliced	¼ teaspoon pepper, or to taste
2 celery ribs, sliced	1 bay leaf (optional)
1 large onion, chopped	½ teaspoon liquid barbecue smoke (optional)

1. Empty beans into 5.7-litre slow cooker or divide ingredients between 2 (3.8 to 4.8-litre) cookers.
2. Cover. Cook on low while preparing vegetables.
3. Cook broth or stock and vegetables in stockpot until vegetables are tender-crisp. Transfer to slow cooker.
4. Add remaining ingredients and mix well.
5. Cover. Cook on low 4 to 5 hours.
6. Serve.

Southwestern Bean Soup with Cornmeal Dumplings

Prep time: 20 minutes | Cook time: 4½ to 12½ hours |
| Serves 4

Soup:	chicken, or vegetable bouillon granules
1 (400 g) can red kidney beans, rinsed and drained	1 to 2 teaspoons chilli powder
1 (400 g) can black beans, pinto beans, or butter beans, rinsed and drained	2 cloves garlic, minced
	Dumplings:
750 ml water	75 g flour
1 (400 g) can Mexican-style stewed tomatoes or underripe tomatoes if unavailable	60 g yellow cornmeal or polenta or semolina
	1 teaspoon baking powder
285 g frozen sweetcorn, thawed	Dash of salt
225 g sliced carrots	Dash of pepper
225 g chopped onions	1 egg white, beaten
115 g chopped green chillies	2 tablespoons milk
2 tablespoons instant beef,	1 tablespoon oil

1. Combine 11 soup ingredients in slow cooker.
2. Cover. Cook on low 10 to 12 hours, or on high 4 to 5 hours.
3. Make dumplings by mixing together flour, cornmeal, baking powder, salt, and pepper.
4. Combine egg white, milk, and oil. Add to flour mixture. Stir with fork until just combined.
5. At the end of the soup's cooking time, turn slow cooker to high. Drop dumpling mixture by rounded teaspoonfuls to make 8 mounds atop the soup.
6. Cover. Cook for 30 minutes (do not lift cover).

Black Bean and Corn Soup

Prep time: 10 minutes | Cook time: 5 to 6 hours |
Serves 6 to 8

2 (400 g) cans black beans, drained and rinsed	300 g sweetcorn, drained
1 (400 g) can Mexican or other chopped tomatoes, undrained	4 spring onions, sliced
	2 to 3 tablespoons chilli powder
1 (400 g) can chopped tomatoes, undrained	1 teaspoon ground cumin
	½ teaspoon dried minced garlic

1. Combine all ingredients in slow cooker.
2. Cover. Cook on high 5 to 6 hours.

Chapter 3 Breads and Sandwiches

Cornbread from Scratch

Prep time: 15 minutes | Cook time: 2 to 3 hours | Serves 6

285 g flour	1 teaspoon salt
175 g yellow cornmeal or polenta or semolina	1 egg, slightly beaten
60 g sugar	250 ml milk
4½ teaspoons baking powder	75 g butter, melted, or oil

1.In mixing bowl sift together flour, cornmeal, sugar, baking powder, and salt. Make a well in the centre.
2.Pour egg, milk, and butter into well. Mix into the dry mixture until just moistened.
3.Pour mixture into a greased 1.9-kg mould. Cover with a plate. Place on a trivet or rack in the bottom of slow cooker.
4.Cover. Cook on high 2 to 3 hours.

Boston Brown Bread

Prep time: 20 minutes | Cook time: 4 hours | Makes 3 loaves

3 (400 g) vegetable cans, cleaned and emptied	1 teaspoon bicarbonate of soda
115 g rye flour	¾ teaspoon salt
115 g yellow cornmeal or polenta or semolina	115 g chopped walnuts
115 g wholemeal flour	115 g raisins
3 tablespoons sugar	250 ml buttermilk
	115 g molasses or black treacle
	Non-stick cooking spray

1.Spray insides of vegetable cans, and one side of 3 (6-inch-square) pieces of foil, with non-stick cooking spray. Set aside.
2.Combine rye flour, cornmeal, wholemeal flour, sugar, bicarbonate of soda, and salt in a large bowl.
3.Stir in walnuts and raisins.
4.Whisk together buttermilk and molasses or black treacle. Add to dry ingredients. Stir until well mixed. Spoon into prepared cans.
5.Place one piece of foil, greased side down, on top of each can. Secure foil with rubber bands or cotton string. Place upright in slow cooker.
6.Pour boiling water into slow cooker to come halfway up sides of cans. (Make sure foil tops do not touch boiling water).
7.Cover cooker. Cook on low 4 hours, or until skewer inserted in centre of bread comes out clean.
8.To remove bread, lay cans on their sides. Roll and tap gently on all sides until bread releases. Cool completely on wire racks.
9.Serve.

Parmesan Garlic Quick Bread

Prep time: 5 minutes | Cook time: 1 hour | Serves 8

350 g low-fat buttermilk baking mix (if unavailable, make your own by adding lemon juice, vinegar or plain yoghurt to milk)	125 ml skimmed milk
	1 tablespoon minced onions
	1 tablespoon sugar
	1½ teaspoons garlic powder
2 egg whites	60 g low-fat Parmesan cheese
	Cooking spray

1.Combine baking mix, egg whites, milk, onions, sugar, and garlic powder in a mixing bowl.
2.Spray slow cooker with cooking spray. Spoon dough into cooker.
3.Sprinkle dough with Parmesan cheese.
4.Cook on high 1 hour.

Cottage Cheese Bread

Prep time: 5 minutes | Cook time: 2 hours | Serves 8

225 g fat-free cottage cheese	mix (if unavailable, make your own by adding lemon juice, vinegar or plain yoghurt to milk)
4 egg whites	
225 g sugar	
175 g fat-free or semi-skimmed milk	115 g raisins or dried cranberries
1 teaspoon vanilla	
625 g low-fat buttermilk baking	½ teaspoon orange zest

1.Combine all ingredients in a mixing bowl.
2.Pour into greased slow cooker.
3.Cook on high 2 hours.

Broccoli Cornbread

Prep time: 15 minutes | Cook time: 6 hours | Serves 8

1 stick butter, melted	mix
285 g chopped broccoli, cooked and drained	4 eggs, well beaten
1 onion, chopped	250 g cottage cheese
1 box cornbread or corn muffin	1¼ teaspoons salt

1.Combine all ingredients. Mix well.
2.Pour into greased slow cooker. Cook on low 6 hours, or until toothpick inserted in centre comes out clean.
3.Serve like spoon bread, or invert the pot, remove bread, and cut into wedges.

Cheery Cherry Bread

Prep time: 15 minutes | Cook time: 2 to 3 hours |
Serves 6 to 8

170 g jar maraschino or glacé cherries	¼ teaspoon salt
	2 eggs
350 g flour	175 g sugar
1½ teaspoons baking powder	175 g coarsely chopped pecans

1. Drain cherries, reserving 75 g syrup. Cut cherries in pieces. Set aside.
2. Combine flour, baking powder, and salt.
3. Beat eggs and sugar together until thickened.
4. Alternately add flour mixture and cherry syrup to egg mixture, mixing until well blended after each addition.
5. Fold in cherries and pecans. Spread in well-greased and floured baking insert or (900 g) coffee can. If using baking insert, cover with its lid; if using a coffee can, cover with 6 layers of paper towels. Set in slow cooker.
6. Cover cooker. Cook on high 2 to 3 hours.
7. Remove from slow cooker. Let stand 10 minutes before removing from pan.
8. Cool before slicing.

Beach Boy's Pot Roast

Prep time: 10 minutes | Cook time: 8 to 12 hours |
Makes 6 to 8 sandwiches

1 (1.4 to 1.8 kg) chuck or top round roast	fragata peppers, undrained
	6 to 8 large sub rolls
8 to 12 slivers of garlic	12 to 16 slices of your favourite cheese
3 (300 g) jar pepperoncini or	

1. Cut slits into roast with a sharp knife and insert garlic slivers.
2. Place beef in slow cooker. Spoon peppers and all of their juice over top.
3. Cover and cook on low 8 to 12 hours, or until meat is tender but not dry.
4. Remove meat from cooker and allow to cool. Then use 2 forks to shred the beef.
5. Spread on sub rolls and top with cheese.

Hot Beef Sandwiches

Prep time: 10 minutes | Cook time: 8 to 10 hours |
Makes 10 sandwiches

1.4 kg beef chuck roast	1 to 1½ teaspoons salt
1 large onion, chopped	¼ to ½ teaspoon pepper
125 ml vinegar	Hamburger buns, for serving
1 clove garlic, minced	

1. Place meat in slow cooker. Top with onions.
2. Combine vinegar, garlic, salt, and pepper. Pour over meat.
3. Cover. Cook on low 8 to 10 hours.
4. Drain broth or stock but save for dipping.
5. Shred meat.
6. Serve on hamburger buns with broth or stock on side.

Beef Pittas

Prep time: 15 minutes | Cook time: 3 to 4 hours |
Makes 2 sandwiches

250 g beef or pork, cut into small cubes	peppers
	60 ml fat-free sour cream
½ teaspoon dried oregano	1 teaspoon red wine vinegar
Dash of black pepper	1 teaspoon vegetable oil
225 g chopped fresh tomatoes	2 large pitta breads, heated and cut in half
2 tablespoons diced fresh green	

1. Place meat in slow cooker. Sprinkle with oregano and black pepper.
2. Cook on low 3 to 4 hours.
3. In a separate bowl, combine tomatoes, green peppers, sour cream, vinegar, and oil.
4. Fill pittas with meat. Top with vegetable and sour cream mixture.

Healthy Wholemeal Bread

Prep time: 20 minutes | Cook time: 2½ to 3 hours |
Serves 8

500 ml warm reconstituted powdered milk	¾ teaspoon salt
	1 package yeast
2 tablespoons vegetable oil	565 g wholemeal flour
60 g honey or brown sugar	285 g white flour

1. Mix together milk, oil, honey or brown sugar, salt, yeast, and half the flour in electric mixer bowl. Beat with mixer for 2 minutes. Add remaining flour. Mix well.
2. Place dough in well-greased bread or cake pan that will fit into your cooker. Cover with greased foil. Let stand for 5 minutes. Place in slow cooker.
3. Cover cooker and cook on high 2½ to 3 hours. Remove pan and uncover. Let stand for 5 minutes. Serve warm.

Tangy Barbecue Sandwiches

Prep time: 20 minutes | Cook time: 7 to 9 hours |
Makes 14 to 18 sandwiches

675 g chopped celery	2 tablespoons brown sugar
225 g chopped onions	1 teaspoon chilli powder
225 g ketchup	1 teaspoon salt
225 g barbecue sauce	½ teaspoon pepper
250 ml water	½ teaspoon garlic powder
2 tablespoons vinegar	1 (1.4 to 1.8 kg) boneless chuck roast
2 tablespoons Worcestershire sauce	14 to 18 hamburger buns

1. Combine all ingredients except roast and buns in slow cooker. When well mixed, add roast.
2. Cover. Cook on high 6 to 7 hours.
3. Remove roast. Cool and shred meat. Return to sauce. Heat well.
4. Serve on buns.

Herby French Sandwiches

Prep time: 5 minutes | Cook time: 5 to 6 hours |
Makes 6 to 8 sandwiches

1 (1.4 kg) chuck roast
500 ml water
115 g soy sauce
1 teaspoon garlic powder
1 bay leaf
3 to 4 whole peppercorns

1 teaspoon dried rosemary
(optional)
1 teaspoon dried thyme
(optional)
6 to 8 French rolls

1. Place roast in slow cooker.
2. Combine remaining ingredients in a mixing bowl. Pour over meat.
3. Cover and cook on high 5 to 6 hours, or until meat is tender but not dry.
4. Remove meat from broth or stock and shred with fork. Stir back into sauce.
5. Remove meat from the cooker by large forkfuls and place on French rolls.

Zesty French Sandwiches

Prep time: 5 minutes | Cook time: 8 hours | Makes 6
to 8 sandwiches

1 (1.8 kg) beef roast
300 ml beef broth or stock
300 g condensed French onion

soup
1 (330 ml) bottle of beer
6 to 8 French rolls or baguettes

1. Pat roast dry and place in slow cooker.
2. In a mixing bowl, combine beef broth or stock, onion soup, and beer. Pour over meat.
3. Cover and cook on low 8 hours, or until meat is tender but not dry.
4. Split rolls or baguettes. Warm in the oven or microwave until heated through.
5. Remove meat from cooker and allow to rest for 10 minutes. Then shred with two forks, or cut on the diagonal into thin slices, and place in rolls. Serve.

Barbecued Beef Sandwiches

Prep time: 10 minutes | Cook time: 10 to 12 hours |
Makes 18 to 20 sandwiches

1 (1.6 to 1.8 kg) beef topside or
silverside steak, cubed
225 g finely chopped onions
115 g firmly packed brown
sugar
1 tablespoon chilli powder

115 g ketchup
75 ml cider vinegar
1 (330 ml) can beer
1 (190 g) tube tomato paste
Buns

1. Combine all ingredients except buns in slow cooker.
2. Cover. Cook on low 10 to 12 hours.
3. Remove beef from sauce with slotted spoon.
4. Place in large bowl. Shred with 2 forks. Add 450 g sauce from slow cooker to shredded beef. Mix well.
5. Pile into buns and serve immediately.

Herby Beef Sandwiches

Prep time: 5 minutes | Cook time: 7 to 8 hours |
Makes 10 to 12 sandwiches

1 (1.4 to 1.8 kg) boneless beef
chuck roast
3 tablespoons fresh basil, or 1
tablespoon dried basil
3 tablespoons fresh oregano, or
1 tablespoon dried oregano

375 ml water
1 package dry onion soup mix
(or combine onion powder with
mixed herbs)
10 to 12 Italian rolls

1. Place roast in slow cooker.
2. Combine basil, oregano, and water. Pour over roast.
3. Sprinkle with onion soup mix.
4. Cover. Cook on low 7 to 8 hours. Shred meat with fork.
5. Serve on Italian rolls.

Wash-Day Sandwiches

Prep time: 10 minutes | Cook time: 6 to 7 hours |
Makes 8 to 10 sandwiches

680 to 900 g lean lamb or beef,
cubed
2 (400 g) cans chickpeas,
drained
2 (400 g) cans white beans,
drained
2 medium onions, peeled and

quartered
950 ml water
1 teaspoon salt
1 tomato, peeled and quartered
1 teaspoon turmeric
3 tablespoons fresh lemon juice
8 to 10 pitta bread pockets

1. Combine ingredients in slow cooker.
2. Cover. Cook on high 6 to 7 hours.
3. Lift stew from cooker with a strainer spoon and stuff in pitta bread pockets.

Lemon Bread

Prep time: 15 minutes | Cook time: 2 to 2¼ hours |
Serves 6

115 g Trex
175 g sugar
2 eggs, beaten
375 g flour
375 g teaspoons baking powder
½ teaspoon salt

125 ml milk
115 g chopped nuts
Grated peel from 1 lemon
Glaze:
60 g powdered sugar
Juice of 1 lemon

1. Cream together Trex and sugar. Add eggs. Mix well.
2. Sift together flour, baking powder, and salt. Add flour mixture and milk alternately to Trex mixture.
3. Stir in nuts and lemon peel.
4. Spoon batter into well greased 900 g coffee can and cover with well-greased tin foil. Place in cooker set on high for 2 to 2¼ hours, or until done. Remove bread from coffee can.
5. Mix together powdered sugar and lemon juice. Pour over loaf.
6. Serve.

Date and Nut Loaf

Prep time: 20 minutes | Cook time: 3½ to 4 hours |
Serves 16

375 ml boiling water	1 teaspoon vanilla
350 g chopped dates	1 tablespoon butter, melted
285 g sugar	565 g flour
1 egg	225 g walnuts, chopped
2 teaspoons bicarbonate of soda	500 ml hot water
½ teaspoon salt	

1. Pour 375 ml boiling water over dates. Let stand 5 to 10 minutes.
2. Stir in sugar, egg, bicarbonate of soda, salt, vanilla, and butter.
3. In separate bowl, combine flour and nuts. Stir into date mixture.
4. Pour into 2 greased (325 g) coffee cans or one baking insert. If using coffee cans, cover with foil and tie. If using baking insert, cover with its lid. Place cans or insert on rack in slow cooker. (If you don't have a rack, use rubber jar rings instead.)
5. Pour hot water around cans, up to half their height.
6. Cover slow cooker tightly. Cook on high 3½ to 4 hours.
7. Remove cans or insert from cooker. Let bread stand in coffee cans or baking insert 10 minutes. Turn out onto cooling rack. Slice to serve.

Banana Loaf

Prep time: 10 minutes | Cook time: 2 to 2½ hours |
Serves 6 to 8

3 very ripe bananas	225 g sugar
115 g butter, softened	225 g flour
2 eggs	1 teaspoon bicarbonate of soda
1 teaspoon vanilla	

1. Combine all ingredients in an electric mixing bowl. Beat 2 minutes or until well blended. Pour into well-greased (900 g) coffee can.
2. Place can in slow cooker. Cover can with 6 layers of paper towels between cooker lid and bread.
3. Cover cooker. Cook on high 2 to 2½ hours, or until toothpick inserted in centre comes out clean. Cool 15 minutes before removing from pan.

Barbecue Sauce and Hamburgers

Prep time: 25 minutes | Cook time: 5 to 6 hours |
Makes 6 sandwiches

420 ml beef gravy	sauce
115 g ketchup	1 tablespoon prepared mustard
115 g chilli sauce	6 grilled hamburger patties
1 tablespoon Worcestershire	6 slices cheese (optional)

1. Combine all ingredients except hamburger patties and cheese slices in slow cooker.
2. Add hamburger patties.
3. Cover. Cook on low 5 to 6 hours.
4. Serve in buns, each topped with a slice of cheese if you like.

Middle-Eastern Sandwiches (for a crowd)

Prep time: 50 minutes | Cook time: 6 to 8 hours |
Makes 10 to 16 sandwiches

1.8 kg boneless beef or venison, cut in ½-inch cubes	Dash of pepper
4 tablespoons cooking oil	125 ml cold water
450 g chopped onions	115 g cornflour
2 garlic cloves, minced	Pitta pocket breads
250 ml dry red wine	450 g shredded lettuce
1 (190 g) tube tomato paste	1 large tomato, seeded and diced
1 teaspoon dried oregano	1 large cucumber, seeded and diced
1 teaspoon dried basil	
½ teaspoon dried rosemary	250 g plain yoghurt
2 teaspoons salt	

1. Brown meat, 450 g at a time, in skillet or frying pan in 1 tablespoon oil. Reserve drippings and transfer meat to slow cooker.
2. Sauté onion and garlic in drippings until tender. Add to meat.
3. Add wine, tomato paste, oregano, basil, rosemary, salt, and pepper.
4. Cover. Cook on low 6 to 8 hours.
5. Turn cooker to high. Combine cornflour and water in small bowl until smooth. Stir into meat mixture. Cook until bubbly and thickened, stirring occasionally.
6. Split pitta breads to make pockets. Fill each with meat mixture, lettuce, tomato, cucumber, and yoghurt.
7. Serve.

Barbecued Ham Sandwiches

Prep time: 7 minutes | Cook time: 5 hours | Makes 4 to 6 sandwiches

450 g chopped turkey ham or chopped honey glazed ham	1 tablespoon vinegar
1 small onion, finely diced	3 tablespoons brown sugar
115 g ketchup	Buns, for serving

1. Place half of meat in greased slow cooker.
2. Combine other ingredients. Pour half of mixture over meat. Repeat layers.
3. Cover. Cook on low 5 hours.
4. Fill buns and serve.

Tangy Sloppy Joes

Prep time: 15 minutes | Cook time: 3 to 10 hours |
Makes 12 sandwiches

1.4 kg minced beef, browned and drained	1 tablespoon Worcestershire sauce
1 onion, finely chopped	1 teaspoon chilli powder
1 green pepper, chopped	¼ teaspoon pepper
500 g tomato sauce	¼ teaspoon garlic powder
175 g ketchup	Rolls, for serving

1. Combine all ingredients except rolls in slow cooker.
2. Cover. Cook on low 8 to 10 hours, or on high 3 to 4 hours.
3. Serve.

Sloppy Joes Italia

Prep time: 15 minutes | Cook time: 3 to 4 hours | Makes 12 sandwiches

680 g minced turkey, browned in non-stick skillet or frying pan
225 g chopped onions
450 g low-salt tomato sauce
225 g fresh mushrooms, sliced
2 tablespoons Splenda

1 to 2 tablespoons Italian seasoning, according to your taste preference
12 reduced-calorie hamburger buns
12 slices low-fat Mozzarella cheese (optional)

1. Place minced turkey, onions, tomato sauce, and mushrooms in slow cooker.
2. Stir in Splenda and Italian seasoning.
3. Cover. Cook on low 3 to 4 hours.
4. Serve 60 g of Sloppy Joe mixture on each bun, topped with cheese, if desired.

Chapter 4 Beef

Gone-All-Day Dinner

Prep time: 15 minutes | Cook time: 6 to 8 hours |
Serves 8

225 g uncooked wild rice, rinsed and drained
225 g chopped celery
225 g chopped carrots
115 g canned mushrooms, drained
1 large onion, chopped

115 g slivered almonds
3 beef bouillon or stock cubes
2½ teaspoons seasoned salt
900 g boneless topside or silverside steak, cut in bite-sized pieces
750 ml water

1. Layer ingredients in slow cooker in order listed. Do not stir.
2. Cover. Cook on low 6 to 8 hours.
3. Stir before serving.

Taters 'n Beef

Prep time: 20 minutes | Cook time: 4¼ to 6¼ hours |
Serves 6 to 8

900 g minced beef, browned
1 teaspoon salt
½ teaspoon pepper
60 g chopped onions

225 g canned tomato soup
6 potatoes, sliced
250 ml milk

1. Combine beef, salt, pepper, onions, and soup.
2. Place a layer of potatoes in bottom of slow cooker. Cover with a portion of the meat mixture. Repeat layers until ingredients are used.
3. Cover. Cook on low 4 to 6 hours. Add milk and cook on high 15 to 20 minutes.

Sour Cream Meatballs

Prep time: 35 minutes | Cook time: 4¼ to 5¼ hours |
Serves 6 to 8

450 g minced beef
250 g minced pork
125 g minced onions
175 g fine dry breadcrumbs
1 tablespoon minced parsley
1 teaspoon salt
⅛ teaspoon pepper
½ teaspoon garlic powder
1 tablespoon Worcestershire sauce
1 egg

125 ml milk
60 ml oil
Gravy:
60 g flour
¼ teaspoon salt
¼ teaspoon garlic powder
⅛ teaspoon pepper
1 teaspoon paprika
500 ml boiling water
175 ml sour cream

1. Combine meats, onions, breadcrumbs, parsley, salt, pepper, garlic powder, Worcestershire sauce, egg, and milk.
2. Shape into balls the size of a walnut. Brown in oil in skillet or frying pan. Reserve drippings, and place meatballs in slow cooker.
3. Cover. Cook on high 10 to 15 minutes.
4. Stir flour, salt, garlic powder, pepper, and paprika into hot drippings in skillet or frying pan. Stir in water and sour cream. Pour over meatballs.
5. Cover. Reduce heat to low. Cook 4 to 5 hours.
6. Serve.

Beef-Vegetable Casserole

Prep time: 20 minutes | Cook time: 4 to 5 hours |
Serves 8

450 g extra-lean minced beef or turkey
1 medium onion, chopped
115 g chopped celery
900 g chopped cabbage
565 g canned stewed tomatoes, slightly mashed

1 tablespoon flour
1 teaspoon salt
1 tablespoon sugar
¼ to ½ teaspoon black pepper, according to your taste preference

1. Sauté meat, onion, and celery in non-stick skillet or frying pan until meat is browned.
2. Pour into slow cooker.
3. Top with layers of cabbage, tomatoes, flour, salt, sugar, and pepper.
4. Cover. Cook on high 4 to 5 hours.

Supper-in-a-Dish

Prep time: 20 minutes | Cook time: 4 hours | Serves 8

450 g minced beef, browned and drained
350 g sliced raw potatoes
225 g sliced carrots
225 g peas
115 g chopped onions
115 g chopped celery

60 g chopped green peppers
1 teaspoon salt
¼ teaspoon pepper
300 g cream of chicken, or mushroom, soup
60 ml milk
150 g shredded mature cheese

1. Layer minced beef, potatoes, carrots, peas, onions, celery, green peppers, salt, and pepper in slow cooker.
2. Combine soup and milk. Pour over layered ingredients. Sprinkle with cheese.
3. Cover. Cook on high 4 hours.

Beef and Lentils

Prep time: 35 minutes | Cook time: 6 to 8 hours |

Serves 12

1 medium onion
3 whole cloves
1.25 litres water
450 g lentils
1 teaspoon salt
1 bay leaf
450 g (or less) minced beef, browned and drained

115 g ketchup
60 g molasses or black treacle
2 tablespoons brown sugar
1 teaspoon dry mustard
¼ teaspoon Worcestershire sauce
1 onion, finely chopped

1.Stick cloves into whole onion. Set aside.
2.In large saucepan, combine water, lentils, salt, bay leaf, and whole onion with cloves. Simmer 30 minutes.
3.Meanwhile, combine all remaining ingredients in slow cooker. Stir in simmered ingredients from saucepan. Add additional water if mixture seems dry.
4.Cover. Cook on low 6 to 8 hours (check to see if lentils are tender).

Courgette Hot Dish

Prep time: 20 minutes | Cook time: 2 to 3 hours |

Serves 4

450 g minced beef
1 small onion, chopped (optional)
Salt and pepper to taste
4 to 5 (6-inch-long) courgettes,

sliced
300 g cream of mushroom soup
225 to 450 g shredded Cheddar cheese

1.Brown minced beef with onions, if you wish, along with salt and pepper in a non-stick skillet or frying pan until crumbly. Drain.
2.Layer courgette and beef mixture alternately in slow cooker.
3.Top with soup. Sprinkle with cheese.
4.Cover and cook on low 2 to 3 hours, or until the courgette is done to your liking.

1-2 to 3-4 Casserole

Prep time: 35 minutes | Cook time: 7 to 9 hours |

Serves 8

450 g minced beef
2 onions, sliced
3 carrots, thinly sliced
4 potatoes, thinly sliced
½ teaspoon salt
⅛ teaspoon pepper

250 ml cold water
½ teaspoon cream of tartar
300 g cream of mushroom soup
60 ml milk
½ teaspoon salt
⅛ teaspoon pepper

1.Layer in greased slow cooker: minced beef, onions, carrots, ½ teaspoon salt, and ⅛ teaspoon pepper.
2.Dissolve cream of tartar in water in bowl. Toss sliced potatoes with water.
3.Drain. Combine soup and milk. Toss with potatoes. Add remaining salt and pepper. Arrange potatoes in slow cooker.
4.Cover. Cook on low 7 to 9 hours.

German Dinner

Prep time: 10 minutes | Cook time: 9 to 11 hours |

Serves 6

900 g sauerkraut, drained
450 g extra-lean minced beef
1 small green pepper, grated

650 ml V-8 juice
115 g chopped celery (optional)

1.Combine all ingredients in slow cooker.
2.Cook for 1 hour on high, and then on low 8 to 10 hours.

Halloween Hash

Prep time: 25 minutes | Cook time: 2 to 4 hours |

Serves 4

450 g lean minced beef
115 g chopped onion
450 g canned sweetcorn, drained
1 (400 g) can kidney beans,

drained
1 (400 g) can chopped tomatoes
115 g shredded Cheddar cheese (optional)

1.Brown beef and onion in a non-stick skillet or frying pan until no longer pink. Drain. Place mixture in your slow cooker.
2.Layer in all remaining ingredients except the cheese.
3.Cover and cook on low 2 to 4 hours, or until thoroughly hot.
4.Sprinkle each serving with cheese, if you wish.

A Hearty Western Casserole

Prep time: 10 minutes | Cook time: 1 hour | Serves 5

450 g minced beef, browned
450 g canned sweetcorn, drained
1 (400 g) can red kidney beans, drained
300 g condensed tomato soup

225 g Colby or Monterey Jack cheese
60 ml milk
1 teaspoon minced dry onion flakes
½ teaspoon chilli powder

1.Combine beef, sweetcorn, beans, soup, cheese, milk, onion, and chilli powder in slow cooker.
2.Cover. Cook on low 1 hour.

Hamburger Potatoes

Prep time: 15 minutes | Cook time: 6 to 8 hours |

Serves 3 to 4

3 medium potatoes, sliced
3 carrots, sliced
1 small onion, sliced
2 tablespoons dry rice
1 teaspoon salt
½ teaspoon pepper

450 g minced beef, browned and drained
375 to 500 ml tomato juice, as needed to keep dish from getting too dry

1.Combine all ingredients in slow cooker.
2.Cover. Cook on low 6 to 8 hours.

Stuffed Green Peppers with Corn

Prep time: 20 minutes | Cook time: 5 to 6 hours |
Serves 6

6 green peppers
250 g extra-lean minced beef
60 g finely chopped onions
1 tablespoon chopped pimento
¾ teaspoon salt
¼ teaspoon black pepper
340 g low-salt canned

sweetcorn, drained
1 tablespoon Worcestershire
sauce
1 teaspoon prepared mustard
300 g condensed low-salt cream
of tomato soup

1. Cut a slice off the top of each pepper.
2. Remove core, seeds, and white membrane. In a small bowl, combine beef, onions, pimento, salt, black pepper, and sweetcorn.
3. Spoon into peppers. Stand peppers up in slow cooker.
4. Combine Worcestershire sauce, mustard, and tomato soup. Pour over peppers.
5. Cover. Cook on low 5 to 6 hours.

Stuffed Green Peppers with Rice

Prep time: 40 minutes | Cook time: 5 to 7 hours |
Serves 6

6 green peppers
450 g minced beef
60 g chopped onions
1 teaspoon salt
¼ teaspoon pepper

285 g rice, cooked
1 tablespoon Worcestershire
sauce
225 g tomato sauce
60 ml beef broth or stock

1. Cut stem ends from peppers. Carefully remove seeds and membrane without breaking pepper apart. Parboil in water for 5 minutes. Drain. Set aside.
2. Brown minced beef and onions in skillet or frying pan. Drain off drippings. Place meat and onions in mixing bowl.
3. Add seasonings, rice, and Worcestershire sauce to meat and combine well. Stuff green peppers with mixture. Stand stuffed peppers upright in large slow cooker.
4. Mix together tomato sauce and beef broth or stock. Pour over peppers.
5. Cover. Cook on low 5 to 7 hours.

Pizza Rice Casserole

Prep time: 20 minutes | Cook time: 6 hours | Serves
6 to 8

450 g minced beef
1 medium onion, chopped
675 g long grain rice, uncooked
950 g pizza sauce

675 g shredded cheese, your
choice of flavour
225 g cottage cheese (optional)
1 litre water

1. Place minced beef and chopped onion in a non-stick skillet or frying pan. Brown and then drain.
2. Mix all ingredients in slow cooker.
3. Cover and cook on high for 6 hours, or until the rice is tender.

Stuffed Cabbage

Prep time: 25 minutes | Cook time: 8 to 10 hours |
Serves 8

1 litre water
12 large cabbage leaves, cut
from head at base and washed
450 g lean minced beef or lamb
115 g rice, cooked
½ teaspoon salt
¼ teaspoon black pepper

¼ teaspoon dried thyme
¼ teaspoon nutmeg
¼ teaspoon cinnamon
1 (190 g) tube tomato paste
175 ml water

1. Boil 1 litre water in saucepan. Turn off heat. Soak cabbage leaves in water for 5 minutes. Remove. Drain. Cool.
2. Combine minced beef, rice, salt, pepper, thyme, nutmeg, and cinnamon.
3. Place 2 tablespoons of mixture on each cabbage leaf. Roll firmly. Stack in slow cooker.
4. Combine tomato paste and 175 ml water.
5. Pour over stuffed cabbage. Cover. Cook on low 8 to 10 hours.

Stuffed Minced beef

Prep time: 10 minutes | Cook time: 4 to 6 hours |
Serves 4

450 g minced beef
450 g shredded cabbage
Salt and pepper to taste

450 g stuffing
500 ml tomato juice

1. Brown minced beef in a non-stick skillet or frying pan. Drain.
2. Spray the inside of the cooker with non-stick cooking spray. Layer ingredients in slow cooker in this order: minced beef, cabbage, salt and pepper, stuffing
3. Pour tomato juice over top.
4. Cook on low 4 to 6 hours, or until cabbage is just tender.

Cedric's Casserole

Prep time: 30 minutes | Cook time: 3 to 4 hours |
Serves 4 to 6

1 medium onion, chopped
3 tablespoons butter or
margarine
450 g minced beef

½ to ¾ teaspoon salt
¼ teaspoon pepper
675 g shredded cabbage
300 g tomato soup

1. Sauté onion in skillet or frying pan in butter.
2. Add minced beef and brown. Season with salt and pepper.
3. Layer half of cabbage in slow cooker, followed by half of meat mixture. Repeat layers.
4. Pour soup over top.
5. Cover. Cook on low 3 to 4 hours.
6. Serve.

Tostadas

Prep time: 15 minutes | Cook time: 6 hours | Serves 6 to 10

450 g minced beef, browned
2 (435 g) cans refried beans
1 envelope dry taco seasoning mix
225 g tomato sauce
125 ml water
10 tostada shells or taco shells

350 g shredded lettuce
2 tomatoes, diced
250 g shredded Cheddar cheese
1 can sliced black olives
475 ml sour cream
Guacamole
Salsa

1. Combine minced beef, refried beans, taco seasoning mix, tomato sauce, and water in slow cooker.
2. Cover. Cook on low 6 hours.
3. Crisp tostada or taco shells.
4. Spread hot mixture on tostada shells. Top with remaining ingredients.

Mexican Cornbread

Prep time: 20 minutes | Cook time: 4½ to 6 hours | Serves 6

450 g cream-style corn or sweetcorn
225 g cornmeal
½ teaspoon bicarbonate of soda
1 teaspoon salt
60 ml oil
250 ml milk
2 eggs, beaten

115 g taco sauce
450 g shredded Cheddar cheese
1 medium onion, chopped
1 garlic clove, minced
1 (113 g) can diced green chillies
450 g minced beef, lightly cooked and drained

1. Combine sweetcorn, cornmeal, bicarbonate of soda, salt, oil, milk, eggs, and taco sauce. Pour half of mixture into slow cooker.
2. Layer cheese, onion, garlic, green chillies, and minced beef on top of cornmeal mixture.
3. Cover with remaining cornmeal mixture. Cover. Cook on high 1 hour and on low 3½ to 4 hours, or only on low 6 hours.

Tamale Pie

Prep time: 10 minutes | Cook time: 4 hours | Serves 8

175 g cornmeal
375 ml milk
1 egg, beaten
450 g minced beef, browned and drained
1 envelope dry chilli seasoning

mix
1 (400 g) can chopped tomatoes
450 g canned sweetcorn, drained
225 g shredded Cheddar cheese

1. Combine cornmeal, milk, and egg.
2. Stir in meat, chilli seasoning mix, tomatoes, and sweetcorn until well blended. Pour into slow cooker.
3. Cover. Cook on high 1 hour, then on low 3 hours.
4. Sprinkle with cheese. Cook another 5 minutes until cheese is melted.

Meal-in-One

Prep time: 25 minutes | Cook time: 4 hours | Serves 6 to 8

900 g minced beef
1 onion, diced
1 green pepper, diced
1 teaspoon salt
¼ teaspoon pepper

1 large bag frozen hash browns
450 ml sour cream
680 g cottage cheese
225 g Monterey Jack cheese, shredded

1. Brown minced beef, onion, and green pepper in skillet or frying pan. Drain. Season with salt and pepper.
2. In slow cooker, layer one-third of the hash browns, meat, sour cream, and cottage cheese. Repeat twice.
3. Cover. Cook on low 4 hours, sprinkling Monterey Jack cheese over top during last hour.
4. Serve.

Bean Tater Tot Casserole

Prep time: 10 minutes | Cook time: 4 hours | Serves 6

450 g minced beef
½ teaspoon salt
¼ teaspoon pepper
1 onion, chopped

450 g frozen string beans
300 g cream of mushroom soup
225 g shredded cheese
600 g frozen potato crunchies

1. Crumble raw minced beef in bottom of slow cooker. Sprinkle with salt and pepper.
2. Layer remaining ingredients on beef in order listed.
3. Cover. Cook on high 1 hour. Reduce heat to low and cook 3 hours.

Meal-in-One-Casserole

Prep time: 20 minutes | Cook time: 4 hours | Serves 4 to 6

450 g minced beef
1 medium onion, chopped
1 medium green pepper, chopped
430 g canned sweetcorn, drained
115 g canned mushrooms, drained

1 teaspoon salt
¼ teaspoon pepper
310 g salsa
1.1 kg egg noodles, uncooked
2 (800 g) can chopped tomatoes, undrained
225 g shredded Cheddar cheese

1. Cook beef and onion in saucepan over medium heat until meat is no longer pink. Drain. Transfer to slow cooker.
2. Top with green pepper, sweetcorn, and mushrooms. Sprinkle with salt and pepper. Pour salsa over mushrooms. Cover and cook on low 3 hours.
3. Cook noodles according to package in separate pan. Drain and add to slow cooker after mixture in cooker has cooked for 3 hours. Top with tomatoes. Sprinkle with cheese.
4. Cover. Cook on low 1 more hour.

Creamy Hamburger Topping

Prep time: 15 minutes | Cook time: 3 to 5 hours |

Serves 8

450 g minced beef
250 g shredded cheese, your choice of flavours
1 onion, diced

300 g cream of mushroom soup
340 g canned chopped tomatoes, undrained

1. Brown minced beef in a non-stick skillet or frying pan. Drain.
2. Combine all ingredients in your slow cooker.
3. Cook on low 3 to 5 hours, or until heated through.
4. Serve.

Minced beef Goulash

Prep time: 10 minutes | Cook time: 5 to 6 hours |

Serves 10

450 g extra-lean minced beef
1 large onion, sliced
1 clove garlic, minced
115 g ketchup
2 tablespoons Worcestershire sauce
1 tablespoon brown sugar

1 to 1½ teaspoons salt
2 teaspoons paprika
½ teaspoon dry mustard
250 ml water
60 g flour
60 ml cold water

1. Place meat in slow cooker. Cover with onions.
2. Combine garlic, ketchup, Worcestershire sauce, sugar, salt, paprika, mustard, and 250 ml water. Pour over meat.
3. Cook on low 5 to 6 hours.
4. Dissolve flour in 60 ml cold water. Stir into meat mixture.
5. Cook on high 10 to 15 minutes, or until slightly thickened.
6. Serve.

Cheese and Pasta in a Pot

Prep time: 40 minutes | Cook time: 2 to 3 hours |

Serves 8

900 g minced beef
1 tablespoon oil
2 medium onions, chopped
1 garlic clove, minced
400 g spaghetti or pasta sauce
1 (400 g) can stewed tomatoes
115 g canned sliced mushrooms,

undrained
250 g dry macaroni, cooked al dente
850 ml sour cream
250 g provolone cheese, sliced
250 g Mozzarella cheese, thinly sliced or shredded

1. Brown minced beef in oil in skillet or frying pan. Drain off all but 2 tablespoons drippings.
2. Add onions, garlic, spaghetti or pasta sauce, stewed tomatoes, and undrained mushrooms to drippings. Mix well. Simmer 20 minutes, or until onions are soft.
3. Pour half of macaroni into slow cooker. Cover with half the tomato/meat sauce. Spread half the sour cream over sauce. Top with provolone cheese. Repeat, ending with Mozzarella cheese.
4. Cover. Cook on high 2 hours, or on low 3 hours.

Shell Casserole

Prep time: 20 minutes | Cook time: 2¼ to 3¼ hours |

Serves 4 to 5

450 g minced beef
1 small onion, chopped
¾ teaspoon salt
¼ teaspoon garlic powder
1 teaspoon Worcestershire sauce
60 g flour
285 ml hot water

2 teaspoons beef bouillon granules
2 tablespoons red wine
170 g medium-sized shell pasta, uncooked
115 g canned sliced mushrooms, drained
250 ml sour cream

1. Brown minced beef and onion in saucepan. Drain. Place in slow cooker.
2. Stir in salt, garlic powder, Worcestershire sauce, and flour.
3. Add water, bouillon, and wine. Mix well.
4. Cover. Cook on low 2 to 3 hours.
5. Cook pasta in separate pan according to package directions. Stir cooked pasta, mushrooms, and sour cream into slow cooker. Cover. Cook on high 10 to 15 minutes.

Beef and Macaroni

Prep time: 20 minutes | Cook time: 2 to 2½ hours |

Serves 4 to 5

450 g minced beef
1 small onion, chopped
Half a green pepper, chopped
115 g macaroni, cooked
½ teaspoon dried basil
½ teaspoon dried thyme

1 teaspoon Worcestershire sauce
1 teaspoon salt
300 g Cheddar cheese soup or alternative such as leek and Cheddar soup

1. Brown beef, onions, and green pepper in skillet or frying pan. Pour off drippings and place meat and vegetables in slow cooker.
2. Combine all ingredients in cooker.
3. Cover. Cook on high 2 to 2½ hours, stirring once or twice.
4. Serve.

Plenty More in the Kitchen

Prep time: 30 minutes | Cook time: 5 hours | Serves

12 to 16

1.4 kg minced beef
225 g chopped onions
1 tablespoon oil
740 g tomato, spaghetti or pasta sauce
1 teaspoon salt
2 teaspoons chilli powder

1 teaspoon pepper
2 tablespoons dark brown sugar
450 g sweetcorn
800 ml beef broth or stock
225 g dry macaroni
225 g shredded mature cheese

1. Brown beef and onion in oil.
2. Combine all ingredients except cheese. Pour into slow cooker.
3. Cover. Cook on high 1 hour. Turn to low and cook 4 more hours.
4. Sprinkle with cheese and cook 10 minutes more.

Easy Beef Tortillas

Prep time: 20 minutes | Cook time: 1½ to 3 hours |
Serves 6

680 g minced beef	450 g salsa
300 g cream of chicken soup	350 g shredded Cheddar cheese
575 g crushed tortilla chips, divided	Non-stick cooking spray

1. Brown minced beef in a non-stick skillet or frying pan. Drain. Stir in soup.
2. Spray inside of cooker with non-stick cooking spray. Sprinkle 350 g tortilla chips in slow cooker. Top with beef mixture, then salsa, and then cheese.
3. Cover and cook on high for 1½ hours, or on low for 3 hours.
4. Sprinkle with remaining chips just before serving.

Tortilla Casserole

Prep time: 20 minutes | Cook time: 3¼ to 4¼ hours |
Serves 4

4 to 6 white or wholemeal tortillas, divided	350 g shredded low-fat cheese of your choice, divided
450 g minced beef	3 to 4 tablespoons sour cream (optional)
1 envelope dry taco seasoning	Non-stick cooking spray
450 g canned fat-free refried beans	

1. Spray the inside of the cooker with non-stick cooking spray. Tear about ¾ of the tortillas into pieces and line the sides and bottom of the slow cooker.
2. Brown the minced beef in a non-stick skillet or frying pan. Drain. Return to skillet or frying pan and mix in taco seasoning.
3. Layer refried beans, browned and seasoned meat, 225 g cheese, and sour cream if you wish, over tortilla pieces.
4. Place remaining tortilla pieces on top.
5. Sprinkle with remaining cheese. Cover and cook on low 3 to 4 hours.

Tamale Casserole

Prep time: 10 minutes | Cook time: 5 to 7 hours |
Serves 6 to 8

900 g frozen meatballs	225 g chopped stuffed green olives
2 (400 g) can chopped tomatoes	
225 g yellow cornmeal, polenta or semolina	½ teaspoon chilli powder (optional)
450 g canned sweetcorn	

1. Microwave frozen meatballs for 4 minutes until thawed. Place in slow cooker. Combine remaining ingredients in a mixing bowl. Pour over meatballs and mix well.
2. Cover and cook on high 1 hour. Turn to low and cook 4 to 6 hours. Check after 4 hours of cooking. The casserole is finished when it reaches a "loaf" consistency.

My Norwegian Meatballs

Prep time: 5 minutes | Cook time: 45 minutes |
Serves 10 to 12

1 (900 g to 1.1 kg) package frozen meatballs	340 g canned evaporated milk
600 to 900 g cream of mushroom soup	375 ml sour cream
	250 ml beef broth or stock
	1 teaspoon dill (optional)

1. Lay frozen meatballs in a long, microwave-safe dish and microwave on high for 4 minutes.
2. Meanwhile, in a large mixing bowl, combine all other ingredients.
3. Place meatballs in slow cooker. Cover with soup mixture.
4. Cover and cook on high 45 minutes (sauce should not boil).
5. Turn to low. Keep warm until serving time.

Beef and Ham Meatballs

Prep time: 20 minutes | Cook time: 2¾ to 3¾ hours |
Serves 5 to 7

680 g minced beef	¼ teaspoon allspice
130 g canned Danish ham	¼ teaspoon pepper
120 ml evaporated milk	60 g flour
2 eggs, beaten slightly	60 ml water
1 tablespoon grated onion	1 tablespoon ketchup
450 g soft breadcrumbs	2 teaspoons dill
1 teaspoon salt	250 ml sour cream

1. Combine beef, ham, milk, eggs, onion, breadcrumbs, salt, allspice, and pepper. Shape into 2-inch meatballs. Arrange in slow cooker.
2. Cover. Cook on low 2½ to 3½ hours. Turn control to high.
3. Dissolve flour in water until smooth. Stir in ketchup and dill. Add to meatballs, stirring gently.
4. Cook on high 15 to 20 minutes, or until slightly thickened.
5. Turn off heat. Stir in sour cream.
6. Serve.

Party Meatballs to Please

Prep time: 50 minutes | Cook time: 3 to 4 hours |
Serves 10 to 12

1.4 kg minced beef	milk
1 package dry onion soup mix (or combine onion powder with mixed herbs)	Sauce:
	510 g ketchup
	125 g brown sugar
400 g sweetened condensed	60 g Worcestershire sauce

1. Combine beef, soup mix, and condensed milk. Form into about 3 dozen meatballs, each about 1½-inches around.
2. Place meatballs on baking sheet.
3. Brown in 350°F (180°C) oven for 30 minutes. Remove from oven and drain. Place meatballs in slow cooker. Combine sauce ingredients. Pour over meatballs.
4. Cover. Cook on low 3 to 4 hours.

Creamy Easy Meatballs

Prep time: 7 minutes | Cook time: 4 to 5 hours |
Serves 10 to 12

600 g cream of mushroom soup	undrained
2 (250 g) packages soft white	250 ml milk
cheese, softened	900 g to 1.4 kg frozen meatballs
115 canned sliced mushrooms,	

1. Combine soup, soft white cheese, mushrooms, and milk in slow cooker.
2. Add meatballs. Stir.
3. Cover. Cook on low 4 to 5 hours.
4. Serve over noodles.

Easy Meatballs for a Group

Prep time: 5 minutes | Cook time: 4 hours | Serves
10 to 12

80 to 100 frozen small	450 g barbecue sauce
meatballs	450 g apricot jam

1. Fill slow cooker with meatballs.
2. Combine sauce and jam. Pour over meatballs.
3. Cover. Cook on low 4 hours, stirring occasionally.
4. Serve as an appetizer, or as a main dish.

Sweet 'n Tangy Meatballs

Prep time: 45 minutes | Cook time: 5 hours | Serves 8

680 g minced beef	60 g ketchup
60 g plain dry breadcrumbs	2 tablespoons honey
3 tablespoons prepared mustard	1 tablespoon red-hot cayenne
1 teaspoon Italian seasoning	pepper sauce
175 g water	20 g packaged brown gravy mix

1. Combine minced beef, breadcrumbs, mustard, and Italian seasoning. Shape into 1-inch balls. Bake or microwave until cooked. Drain. Place meatballs in slow cooker.
2. Cover. Cook on low 3 hours.
3. Combine remaining ingredients in saucepan.
4. Cook for 5 minutes. Pour over meatballs. Cover. Cook on low 2 hours.

Fruity Meatballs

Prep time: 10 minutes | Cook time: 4 to 5 hours |
Serves 8 to 10

900 g frozen meatballs	450 g canned crushed pineapple
225 g brown sugar	with juice

1. Combine ingredients in slow cooker.
2. Cover and cook on low 4 to 5 hours. If you're home and able, stir every 2 hours.

Savoury Meat Loaf

Prep time: 20 minutes | Cook time: 7 hours | Serves
6 to 8

Meat Loaf:	1 tablespoon Worcestershire
900 g minced beef or turkey	sauce
225 g dry rolled oats	1 teaspoon salt
Tomato juice (just enough to	Sauce:
moisten meat if needed)	600 to 740 g mushroom soup
2 eggs	6 to 10 fresh mushrooms, diced
1 onion, diced	1 tablespoon onion flakes
1 tablespoon prepared mustard	Half soup can water
1 teaspoon garlic salt	¼ teaspoon salt
2 tablespoons ketchup	⅛ teaspoon pepper

1. Combine all meat loaf ingredients. Shape into either a round or an oval loaf, to fit the shape of your slow cooker, and place in greased cooker.
2. Cover. Cook on high 1 hour.
3. Combine sauce ingredients. Pour over meat loaf.
4. Cover. Cook on low 6 hours.

A-Touch-of-Italy Meat Loaf

Prep time: 10 minutes | Cook time: 2½ to 6 hours |
Serves 8

900 g minced beef	¼ teaspoon pepper
450 g soft breadcrumbs	1¼ teaspoons salt
115 g spaghetti or pasta sauce	1 teaspoon garlic salt
plus 2 tablespoons, divided	½ teaspoon dried Italian herbs
1 large egg	¼ teaspoon garlic powder
2 tablespoons dried onion	

1. Fold a 30-inch-long piece of foil in half lengthwise. Place in bottom of slow cooker with both ends hanging over the edge of cooker. Grease foil.
2. Combine beef, breadcrumbs, 115 g spaghetti or pasta sauce, egg, onion, and seasonings. Shape into loaf. Place on top of foil in slow cooker. Spread 2 tablespoons spaghetti or pasta sauce over top.
3. Cover. Cook on high 2½ to 3 hours, or on low 5 to 6 hours.

Meat Loaf Sensation

Prep time: 10 minutes | Cook time: 8 to 10 hours |
Serves 8

1.1 kg minced beef	225 g breadcrumbs
115 g salsa	340 g shredded Mexican-mix or
1 package dry taco seasoning,	chilli cheese
divided	2 teaspoons salt
1 egg, slightly beaten	½ teaspoon pepper

1. Combine all ingredients, except half of taco seasoning. Mix well. Shape into loaf and place in slow cooker. Sprinkle with remaining taco seasoning.
2. Cover. Cook on low 8 to 10 hours.

Casserole Verde

Prep time: 35 minutes | Cook time: 4 hours | Serves 6

450 g minced beef	1 (250 g) container cottage
1 small onion, chopped	cheese
⅛ teaspoon garlic powder	1 (113 g) can chopped green
225 g tomato sauce	chillies
75 g chopped black olives	340 g package tortilla chips
115 g canned sliced mushrooms	250 g Monterey Jack cheese,
225 ml sour cream	shredded

1.Brown minced beef, onions, and garlic powder in skillet or frying pan. Drain. Add tomato sauce, olives, and mushrooms.
2.In a separate bowl, combine sour cream, cottage cheese, and green chillies.
3.In slow cooker, layer a third of the chips, and half the minced beef mixture, half the sour cream mixture, and half the shredded cheese. Repeat all layers, except reserve last third of the chips to add just before serving.
4.Cover. Cook on low 4 hours.
5.Ten minutes before serving time, scatter reserved chips over top and continue cooking, uncovered.

Tijuana Tacos

Prep time: 20 minutes | Cook time: 2 hours | Serves 6

675 g cooked chopped beef	¼ teaspoon paprika
1 (435 g) can refried beans	⅛ teaspoon celery salt
115 g chopped onions	⅛ teaspoon ground nutmeg
115 g chopped green peppers	175 ml water
115 g chopped ripe olives	1 teaspoon salt
225 g tomato sauce	225 g crushed corn chips
3 teaspoons chilli powder	6 taco shells
1 tablespoon Worcestershire	Shredded lettuce
sauce	Chopped tomatoes
½ teaspoon garlic powder	Shredded Cheddar cheese
¼ teaspoon pepper	

1.Combine first 15 ingredients in slow cooker.
2.Cover. Cook on high 2 hours.
3.Just before serving, fold in corn chips.
4.Spoon mixture into taco shells. Top with lettuce, tomatoes, and cheese.

Spanish Rice

Prep time: 15 minutes | Cook time: 6 to 10 hours |
Serves 8

900 g minced beef, browned	2½ teaspoons chilli powder
2 medium onions, chopped	2 teaspoons salt
2 green peppers, chopped	2 teaspoons Worcestershire
2 (400 g) can tomatoes	sauce
225 g tomato sauce	350 g rice, uncooked
375 ml water	

1.Combine all ingredients in slow cooker.
2.Cover. Cook on low 8 to 10 hours, or on high 6 hours.

Meatballs and Spaghetti or pasta sauce

Prep time: 35 minutes | Cook time: 6 to 8 hours |
Serves 6 to 8

Meatballs:	300 g tomato soup
680 g minced beef	60 to 115 g grated Romano or
2 eggs	Parmesan cheese
225 g breadcrumbs	1 teaspoon oil
Oil	1 garlic clove, minced
Sauce:	Sliced mushrooms (either
800 g tomato purée	canned or fresh) (optional)
1 (190 g) tube tomato paste	

1.Combine minced beef, eggs, and breadcrumbs. Form into 16 meatballs. Brown in oil in skillet or frying pan.
2.Combine sauce ingredients in slow cooker. Add meatballs. Stir together gently.
3.Cover. Cook on low 6 to 8 hours. Add mushrooms 1 to 2 hours before sauce is finished.
4.Serve.

Nutritious Meat Loaf

Prep time: 10 minutes | Cook time: 3 to 4 hours |
Serves 6

450 g minced beef	1 tablespoon dried onion flakes
450 g finely shredded cabbage	½ teaspoon caraway seeds
1 medium green pepper, diced	1 teaspoon salt

1.Combine all ingredients. Shape into loaf and place on rack in slow cooker.
2.Cover. Cook on high 3 to 4 hours.

Meat Loaf and Mexico

Prep time: 15 minutes | Cook time: 4 to 4½ hours |
Serves 6

565 g extra-lean minced beef	2 tablespoons low-salt taco
900 g hash browns, thawed	seasoning
1 egg, lightly beaten, or egg	450 g fat-free shredded Cheddar
substitute	cheese, divided
2 tablespoons dry vegetable	Fat-free cooking spray
soup mix	

1.Mix together minced beef, hash browns, egg, soup mix, taco seasoning, and 225 g of cheese. Shape into loaf.
2.Line slow cooker with tin foil, allowing ends of foil to extend out over edges of cooker, enough to grab hold of and to lift the loaf out when it's finished cooking. Spray the foil with fat-free cooking spray.
3.Place loaf in cooker. Cover. Cook on low 4 hours.
4.Sprinkle with remaining cheese and cover until melted.
5.Gently lift loaf out, using foil handles. Allow to rest 10 minutes, then slice and serve.

Mexican Chilli Mix and Fritos

Prep time: 15 minutes | Cook time: 4 hours | Serves 4 to 6

450 g minced beef	seasoning
450 g canned cream-style corn, drained or canned sweetcorn	Corn chips
	Shredded cheese (optional)
115 g chunky picante sauce	Chopped olives (optional)
1 (400 g) can pinto or black beans, drained	Sour cream (optional)
	Salsa (optional)
Half an envelope dry taco	

1. Brown minced beef in a large non-stick skillet or frying pan. Drain.
2. Mix beef, corn, picante sauce, beans, and taco seasoning in slow cooker.
3. Cover and cook on low 4 hours.
4. Serve over corn chips with optional garnishes of shredded cheese, chopped olives, sour cream, and salsa.

Chilli con Carne

Prep time: 15 minutes | Cook time: 5 to 6 hours | Serves 8

450 g minced beef	1 (400 g) can kidney beans, drained
225 g chopped onions	
175 g chopped green peppers	225 g tomato sauce
1 garlic clove, minced	2 teaspoons chilli powder
1 (400 g) can tomatoes, cut up	½ teaspoon dried basil

1. Brown beef, onion, green pepper, and garlic in saucepan. Drain.
2. Combine all ingredients in slow cooker.
3. Cover. Cook on low 5 to 6 hours.
4. Serve.

Quick and Easy Chilli

Prep time: 20 minutes | Cook time: 4 to 5 hours | Serves 4

450 g minced beef	1 tablespoon chilli powder
1 onion, chopped	For Garnish:
1 (400 g) can stewed tomatoes	Sour cream
325 ml Hot V-8 juice	Chopped spring onions
2 (400 g) cans pinto beans	Shredded cheese
¼ teaspoon cayenne pepper	Sliced ripe olives
½ teaspoon salt	

1. Crumble minced beef in microwave-safe casserole. Add onion. Microwave, covered, on high 15 minutes. Drain. Break meat into pieces.
2. Combine all ingredients except garnish ingredients in slow cooker.
3. Cook on low 4 to 5 hours.
4. Garnish with sour cream, chopped spring onions, shredded cheese, and sliced ripe olives.

Classic Beef Chilli

Prep time: 15 minutes | Cook time: 4 to 5 hours | Serves 6

450 g extra-lean minced beef	rinsed and drained
2 cloves garlic, chopped finely	1 onion, chopped
2 tablespoons chilli powder	1 (113 g) can diced chillies, undrained
1 teaspoon ground cumin	
2 (400 g) cans chopped tomatoes	2 tablespoons tomato paste
	Fresh oregano sprigs for garnish
1 (400 g) can red kidney beans,	

1. In a large non-stick skillet or frying pan, brown beef and garlic over medium heat. Stir to break up meat. Add chilli powder and cumin. Stir to combine.
2. Mix together tomatoes, beans, onion, chillies, and tomato paste in slow cooker. Add beef mixture and mix thoroughly.
3. Cook on high 4 to 5 hours, or until flavours are well blended.
4. Garnish with oregano to serve.

Slow Cooker Chilli

Prep time: 25 minutes | Cook time: 6 to 12 hours | Serves 8 to 10

1.4 kg stewing steak, browned	½ teaspoon dried oregano
2 cloves garlic, minced	1 tablespoon chilli powder
¼ teaspoon pepper	200 g canned green chillies, chopped
½ teaspoon cumin	
¼ teaspoon dry mustard	1 (400 g) can stewed tomatoes, chopped
210 g jalapeño relish or tomato and jalapeño relish	
	425 g tomato sauce
250 ml beef broth or stock	2 (400 g) cans red kidney beans, rinsed and drained
1 to 1½ onions, chopped, according to your taste preference	2 (400 g) cans pinto beans, rinsed and drained
½ teaspoon salt	

1. Combine all ingredients except kidney and pinto beans in slow cooker.
2. Cover. Cook on low 10 to 12 hours, or on high 6 to 7 hours. Add beans halfway through cooking time.
3. Serve.

Chilli Spaghetti

Prep time: 25 minutes | Cook time: 4 hours | Serves 8 to 10

115 g diced onions	175 g shredded mild cheese
500 ml tomato juice	680 g minced beef, browned
2 teaspoons chilli powder	340 g dry spaghetti, cooked
1 teaspoon salt	

1. Combine all ingredients in slow cooker.
2. Cover. Cook on low 4 hours. Check mixture about halfway through the cooking time. If it's becoming dry, stir in an additional 250 ml of tomato juice.

Dried Beef and Noodles Casserole

Prep time: 5 minutes | Cook time: 3 to 3½ hours |
Serves 4

225 g dry noodles
300 g cream of mushroom soup
250 ml milk

115 g dried beef, shredded
225 g shredded cheese
(optional)

1. Cook noodles as directed on package. Drain and rinse with cold water.
2. In a mixing bowl, blend soup and milk together.
3. Spray the interior of the cooker. Layer ingredients in cooker in this order: cooked noodles, soup-milk mixture, dried beef.
4. Cover and cook on low for 2½ to 3 hours. Sprinkle cheese over top, if you wish. Cover and continue cooking another half hour.

Shredded Beef for Tacos

Prep time: 15 minutes | Cook time: 6 to 8 hours |
Serves 6 to 8

1 (900 g to 1.4 kg) round roast,
cut into large chunks
1 large onion, chopped
3 tablespoons oil
2 serrano or jalapeño chillies,

chopped
3 garlic cloves, minced
1 teaspoon salt
250 ml water

1. Brown meat and onion in oil. Transfer to slow cooker.
2. Add chillies, garlic, salt, and water.
3. Cover. Cook on high 6 to 8 hours.
4. Pull meat apart with two forks until shredded.
5. Serve.

Slow-Cooked Steak Fajitas

Prep time: 25 minutes | Cook time: 8½ to 9½ hours |
Serves 12

680 g beef flank or bavette
steak
1 (400 g) can low-salt chopped
tomatoes with garlic and onion,
undrained
1 jalapeño pepper, seeded and
chopped
2 garlic cloves, minced
1 teaspoon ground coriander
1 teaspoon ground cumin
1 teaspoon chilli powder
½ teaspoon salt
2 medium onions, sliced

2 medium green peppers,
julienned
2 medium sweet red peppers,
julienned
1 tablespoon minced fresh
parsley
2 teaspoons cornflour
1 tablespoon water
12 (6-inch) flour tortillas,
warmed
175 ml fat-free sour cream
175 g low-salt salsa

1. Slice steak thinly into strips across grain. Place in slow cooker.
2. Add tomatoes, jalapeño, garlic, coriander, cumin, chilli powder, and salt.
3. Cover. Cook on low 7 hours.
4. Add onions, peppers, and parsley.
5. Cover. Cook 1 to 2 hours longer, or until meat is tender.
6. Combine cornflour and water until smooth. Gradually stir into

slow cooker.
7. Cover. Cook on high 30 minutes, or until slightly thickened.
8. Using a slotted spoon, spoon about 115 g of meat mixture down the centre of each tortilla.
9. Add 1 tablespoon sour cream and 1 tablespoon salsa to each.
10. Fold bottom of tortilla over filling and roll up.

Southwestern Flair

Prep time: 5 minutes | Cook time: 9 hours | Serves 8
to 12

1 (1.4 to 1.8 kg) chuck roast or
flank or bavette steak
1 envelope dry taco seasoning
225 g chopped onions

1 tablespoon white vinegar
60 g green chillies
Flour tortillas

1. Combine meat, taco seasoning, onions, vinegar, and chillies in slow cooker.
2. Cover. Cook on low 9 hours.
3. Shred meat with fork.
4. Serve with tortillas.

China Dish

Prep time: 20 minutes | Cook time: 6 to 8 hours |
Serves 6

680 g extra-lean minced beef
300 g cream of chicken soup
300 g 98% fat-free cream of
mushroom soup
875 ml water

450 g chopped celery
450 g chopped onions
225 g brown rice, uncooked
3 tablespoons Worcestershire
sauce

1. Brown minced beef in a non-stick skillet or frying pan.
2. Combine all ingredients in slow cooker.
3. Cover. Cook on low 6 to 8 hours.

Beef Enchiladas

Prep time: 15 minutes | Cook time: 4 to 5 hours |
Serves 12 to 16

1 (1.8 kg) boneless chuck roast
2 tablespoons oil
900 g sliced onions
2 teaspoons salt
2 teaspoons black pepper
2 teaspoons cumin seeds
250 g peeled, diced green
chillies

1 (400 g) can peeled, chopped
tomatoes
8 large tortillas (10 to 12-inch
size)
450 g Cheddar cheese, shredded
900 g green or red enchilada
sauce

1. Brown roast on all sides in oil in saucepan. Place roast in slow cooker.
2. Add remaining ingredients except tortillas, cheese, and sauce.
3. Cover. Cook on high 4 to 5 hours.
4. Shred meat with fork and return to slow cooker.
5. Warm tortillas in oven. Heat enchilada sauce. Fill each tortilla with 175 g beef mixture and 115 g cheese. Roll up and serve with sauce.

Taco Casserole

Prep time: 25 minutes | Cook time: 7 to 8 hours | Serves 6

680 g minced beef, browned
1 (400 g) can chopped tomatoes with chillies
300 g cream of onion soup
1 package dry taco seasoning mix
60 ml water

6 corn tortillas, cut in ½-inch strips
125 ml sour cream
225 g shredded Cheddar cheese
2 spring onions, sliced (optional)

1. Combine beef, tomatoes, soup, seasoning mix, and water in slow cooker.
2. Stir in tortilla strips.
3. Cover. Cook on low 7 to 8 hours.
4. Spread sour cream over casserole. Sprinkle with cheese.
5. Cover. Let stand 5 minutes until cheese melts.
6. Remove cover. Garnish with spring onions. Allow to stand for 15 more minutes before serving.

BBQ Meatballs

Prep time: 20 minutes | Cook time: 7 to 10 hours | Serves 12 to 15

Meatballs:
1.4 kg minced beef
140 g canned evaporated milk
225 g dry oatmeal (rolled or instant)
225 g cracker crumbs
2 eggs
115 g chopped onions
½ teaspoon garlic powder

2 teaspoons salt
½ teaspoon pepper
2 teaspoons chilli powder
Sauce:
450 g ketchup
225 g brown sugar
1½ teaspoons liquid smoke
½ teaspoon garlic powder
60 g chopped onions

1. Combine all meatball ingredients.
2. Shape into walnut-sized balls. Place on waxed paper-lined baking sheets. Freeze. When fully frozen, place in plastic bag and store in freezer until needed. When ready to use, place frozen meatballs in slow cooker. Cover. Cook on high as you mix up sauce.
3. Pour combined sauce ingredients over meatballs. Stir.
4. Cover. Continue cooking on high 1 hour. Stir. Turn to low and cook 6 to 9 hours.

Saucy Barbecued Meatballs

Prep time: 30 minutes | Cook time: 5 hours | Serves 10

Meatballs:
340 g minced beef
175 g breadcrumbs
1½ tablespoons minced onion
½ teaspoon horseradish
3 drops Tabasco sauce
2 eggs, beaten
¾ teaspoon salt
½ teaspoon pepper
Butter

Sauce:
175 g ketchup
125 ml water
60 ml cider vinegar
2 tablespoons brown sugar
1 tablespoon minced onion
2 teaspoons horseradish
1 teaspoon salt
1 teaspoon dry mustard
3 drops Tabasco

Dash pepper

1. Combine all meatball ingredients except butter.
2. Shape into ¾-inch balls. Brown in butter in skillet or frying pan. Place in slow cooker. Combine all sauce ingredients. Pour over meatballs.
3. Cover. Cook on low 5 hours.

Festive Cocktail Meatballs

Prep time: 35 minutes | Cook time: 4 hours | Serves 6

900 g minced beef
75 g ketchup
3 teaspoons dry breadcrumbs
1 egg, beaten
2 teaspoons onion flakes
¾ teaspoon garlic salt
½ teaspoon pepper

225 g ketchup
225 g packed brown sugar
1 (190 g) can tomato paste
60 ml soy sauce
60 ml cider vinegar
1 to 1½ teaspoons hot pepper sauce

1. Combine minced beef, 75 g ketchup, breadcrumbs, egg, onion flakes, garlic salt, and pepper. Mix well. Shape into 1-inch meatballs. Place on jelly roll pan. Bake at 350ºF (180ºC) for 18 minutes, or until brown. Place in slow cooker.
2. Combine 225 g ketchup, brown sugar, tomato paste, soy sauce, vinegar, and hot pepper sauce. Pour over meatballs.
3. Cover. Cook on low 4 hours.

Quick-and-Easy Sweet and Sour Meatballs

Prep time: 15 minutes | Cook time: 2 hours | Serves 8 to 10

900 g precooked meatballs
225 g grape or strawberry jam

500 ml cocktail or Mary Rose sauce

1. Place precooked meatballs in your slow cooker.
2. In a medium-sized bowl, mix jam and cocktail sauce together with a whisk (it will be a little lumpy).
3. Pour jam and cocktail sauce over meatballs. Stir well.
4. Cook on high 1 to 2 hours, or until the sauce is heated through.
5. Turn heat to low until you're ready to serve.

Easy Crock Taco Filling

Prep time: 20 minutes | Cook time: 6 to 8 hours | Serves 4 to 6

1 large onion, chopped
450 g minced beef
2 (400 g) cans chilli beans
425 canned Santa Fe, or Mexican, or Fiesta sweetcorn

175 ml water
¼ teaspoon cayenne pepper (optional)
½ teaspoon garlic powder (optional)

1. Brown minced beef and chopped onion in a non-stick skillet or frying pan. Drain.
2. Mix all ingredients together in the slow cooker, blending well.
3. Cover and cook on low for 6 to 8 hours.

Party Meatball Subs

Prep time: 15 minutes | Cook time: 8 to 10 hours |
Serves 30

1 (4.5 kg) bag prepared
meatballs
1 large onion, sliced
10 good-sized fresh
mushrooms, sliced

1.6 kg spaghetti or pasta sauce,
your choice of flavours
2 cloves garlic, minced
450 g Mozzarella cheese,
shredded (optional)

1.Combine all ingredients except the cheese in your slow cooker.
Stir well to coat the meatballs with sauce.
2.Cover and cook on low 8 to 10 hours, stirring occasionally
throughout cooking time to mix juices.
3.Sprinkle Mozzarella cheese and serve, if you wish.

Meatball Stew

Prep time: 25 minutes | Cook time: 4 to 5 hours |
Serves 8

900 g minced beef
½ teaspoon salt
½ teaspoon pepper
6 medium potatoes, cubed
1 large onion, sliced
6 medium carrots, sliced
225 g ketchup

250 ml water
1½ teaspoons balsamic vinegar
1 teaspoon dried basil
1 teaspoon dried oregano
½ teaspoon salt
½ teaspoon pepper

1.Combine beef, ½ teaspoon salt, and ½ teaspoon pepper. Mix well.
Shape into 1-inch balls. Brown meatballs in saucepan over medium
heat. Drain.
2.Place potatoes, onion, and carrots in slow cooker. Top with
meatballs.
3.Combine ketchup, water, vinegar, basil, oregano, ½ teaspoon salt,
and ½ teaspoon pepper. Pour over meatballs.
4.Cover. Cook on high 4 to 5 hours, or until vegetables are tender.

Magic Meat Loaf

Prep time: 20 minutes | Cook time: 9 to 11 hours |
Serves 6

1 egg, beaten
60 ml milk
1½ teaspoons salt
2 slices bread, crumbled
680 g minced beef
Half a small onion, chopped
2 tablespoons chopped green

peppers
2 tablespoons chopped celery
Ketchup
Green pepper rings
4 to 6 potatoes, cubed
3 tablespoons butter, melted

1.Combine egg, milk, salt, and breadcrumbs in large bowl.
2.Allow breadcrumbs to soften. Add meat, onions, green peppers,
and celery. Shape into loaf and place off to the side in slow cooker.
3.Top with ketchup and green pepper rings.
4.Toss potatoes with melted butter. Spoon into cooker alongside
meat loaf.
5.Cover. Cook on high 1 hour, then on low 8 to 10 hours.

Tastes-Like-Turkey

Prep time: 15 minutes | Cook time: 3 to 8 hours |
Serves 6

900 g hamburgers, browned
1 teaspoon salt
½ teaspoon pepper
600 g cream of chicken soup
300 g can cream of celery soup

950 ml milk
1 large package bread stuffing
or large loaf of bread, torn in
pieces

1.Combine all ingredients in large buttered slow cooker.
2.Cover. Cook on high 3 hours, or on low 6 to 8 hours.

Pecos River Red-Frito Pie

Prep time: 10 minutes | Cook time: 8 to 10 hours |
Serves 6

1 large onion, chopped coarsely
1.4 kg coarsely ground
hamburgers
2 garlic cloves, minced
3 tablespoons ground hot red
chilli peppers

2 tablespoons ground mild red
chilli peppers
375 ml water
Corn chips
Shredded Monterey Jack cheese
Shredded Cheddar cheese

1.Combine onion, hamburger, garlic, chillies, and water in slow
cooker.
2.Cover. Cook on low 8 to 10 hours. Drain.
3.Serve over corn chips. Top with mixture of Monterey Jack and
Cheddar cheeses.

Slow Cooker Enchiladas

Prep time: 30 minutes | Cook time: 5 to 7 hours |
Serves 6

450 g lean minced beef
225 g onions, chopped
115 g green pepper, chopped
1 400 g) can pinto or kidney
beans, rinsed and drained
285 g canned chopped tomatoes
and green chillies
250 ml water
1 teaspoon chilli powder
1 (400 g) can black beans,
rinsed and drained

½ teaspoon ground cumin
½ teaspoon salt
¼ teaspoon black pepper
Dash of dried red pepper flakes
and/or several drops Tabasco
sauce (optional)
225 g shredded low-fat extra
mature Cheddar cheese
225 g shredded low-fat
Monterey Jack cheese
6 flour tortillas (6 or 7 inches)

1.In a non-stick skillet or frying pan, brown beef, onions, and green
pepper.
2.Add remaining ingredients, except cheeses and tortillas. Bring to
a boil.
3.Reduce heat. Cover and simmer for 10 minutes.
4.Combine cheeses in a bowl.
5.In slow cooker, layer about 175 g beef mixture, one tortilla, and
about 60 g cheese. Repeat layers until all ingredients are used.
6.Cover. Cook on low 5 to 7 hours.

Extra Easy Chilli

Prep time: 10 minutes | Cook time: 4 to 8 hours |
Serves 4 to 6

450 g minced beef or turkey, uncooked
1 envelope dry chilli seasoning mix
1 (400 g) can chilli beans in

sauce
4 (400 g) cans crushed or chopped tomatoes seasoned with garlic and onion

1. Crumble meat in bottom of slow cooker.
2. Add remaining ingredients. Stir.
3. Cover. Cook on high 4 to 6 hours, or on low 6 to 8 hours. Stir halfway through cooking time.
4. Serve.

Beef and Pepper Rice

Prep time: 20 minutes | Cook time: 3 to 6 hours |
Serves 4 to 6

450 g minced beef
2 green peppers, or 1 green and 1 red pepper, coarsely chopped
225 g chopped onions
225 g brown rice, uncooked

2 beef bouillon or stock cubes, crushed
750 ml water
1 tablespoon soy sauce

1. Brown beef in skillet or frying pan. Drain.
2. Combine all ingredients in slow cooker. Mix well.
3. Cover. Cook on low 5 to 6 hours or on high 3 hours, or until liquid is absorbed.

Hearty Rice Casserole

Prep time: 25 minutes | Cook time: 6 to 7 hours |
Serves 12 to 16

300 g cream of mushroom soup
300 g creamy onion soup
300 g cream of chicken soup
250 ml water
450 g minced beef, browned

450 g pork sausages, browned
1 large onion, chopped
1 large green pepper, chopped
350 g long grain rice
Shredded cheese (optional)

1. Combine all ingredients except cheese in slow cooker. Mix well.
2. Cover. Cook on low 6 to 7 hours, sprinkling with cheese during last hour, if you wish.

Chilli and Cheese on Rice

Prep time: 15 minutes | Cook time: 4 hours | Serves 6

450 g minced beef
1 onion, diced
1 teaspoon dried basil
1 teaspoon dried oregano
1 (400 g) can light red kidney

beans
1 (400 g) can chilli beans
475 g stewed tomatoes, drained
Rice, cooked
Shredded Cheddar cheese

1. Brown minced beef and onion in skillet or frying pan. Season

with basil and oregano.
2. Combine all ingredients except rice and cheese in slow cooker.
3. Cover. Cook on low 4 hours.
4. Serve over cooked rice. Top with cheese.

Chilli Haystacks

Prep time: 20 minutes | Cook time: 1 to 3 hours |
Serves 10 to 12

900 g minced beef, browned
1 small onion, chopped
225 g tomato sauce
2 (400 g) cans chilli beans with chilli gravy, or red beans
550 g mild enchilada sauce, or

mild salsa
½ teaspoon chilli powder
1 teaspoon garlic salt
Pepper to taste
Rice or baked potatoes

1. Combine beef, onion, tomato sauce, chilli beans, enchilada sauce, chilli powder, garlic salt, and pepper. Pour into slow cooker.
2. Cover. Cook on low 2 to 3 hours, or on high 1 hour.
3. Serve over baked potatoes.

African Beef Curry

Prep time: 20 minutes | Cook time: 6 to 8 hours |
Serves 6

450 g extra-lean minced beef, browned
1 large onion, thinly sliced
1 green pepper, diced
1 tomato, peeled and diced

1 apple, peeled, cored, and diced
1 to 2 teaspoons curry (or more to taste)
900 g prepared rice

1. Spray slow cooker with fat-free cooking spray.
2. Add all ingredients except rice in slow cooker and mix well.
3. Cover and cook on high 6 to 8 hours.
4. Serve over hot rice.

Beef and Noodle Casserole

Prep time: 20 minutes | Cook time: 4 hours | Serves 10

450 g extra-lean minced beef
1 medium onion, chopped
1 medium green pepper, chopped
480 g canned sweetcorn, drained
115 g canned mushroom stems and pieces, drained
1 teaspoon salt

¼ teaspoon black pepper
315 g salsa
1.1 kg dry medium egg noodles, cooked
2 (400 g) can low-salt chopped tomatoes, undrained
225 g low-fat shredded Cheddar cheese

1. Brown minced beef and onion in non-stick skillet or frying pan over medium heat. Transfer to slow cooker.
2. Top with remaining ingredients in order listed.
3. Cover. Cook on low 4 hours.

Pork and Beef Barbecue

Prep time: 15 minutes | Cook time: 6 to 8 hours | Serves 14

225 g tomato sauce
115 g brown sugar, packed
60 g chilli powder, or less
60 ml cider vinegar
2 teaspoons Worcestershire sauce
1 teaspoon salt

450 g lean stewing steak, cut into ¾-inch cubes
450 g lean pork tenderloin, cut into ¾-inch cubes
3 green peppers, chopped
3 large onions, chopped

1. Combine tomato sauce, brown sugar, chilli powder, cider vinegar, Worcestershire sauce, and salt in slow cooker.
2. Stir in meats, green peppers, and onions.
3. Cover. Cook on high 6 to 8 hours.
4. Shred meat with two forks. Stir all ingredients together well.
5. Serve.

Slow Cooker Cola Beef

Prep time: 5 minutes | Cook time: 8 to 10 hours | Serves 12

1 (900 g to 1.4 kg) chuck roast, cubed
1 package dry onion soup mix

(or combine onion powder with mixed herbs)
1 (330 ml) can cola

1. Place meat in slow cooker.
2. Sprinkle soup mix over meat. Pour cola over all.
3. Cover. Cook on low 8 to 10 hours.
4. Serve.

Meat Loaf and Mushrooms

Prep time: 20 minutes | Cook time: 5 hours | Serves 6

2 (28 g) slices wholemeal bread
250 g extra-lean minced beef
340 g fat-free minced turkey
350 g mushrooms, sliced
115 g minced onions
1 teaspoon Italian seasoning

¾ teaspoon salt
2 eggs
1 clove garlic, minced
3 tablespoons ketchup
1½ teaspoons Dijon mustard
⅛ teaspoon ground red pepper

1. Fold two strips of tin foil, each long enough to fit from the top of the cooker, down inside and up the other side, plus a 2-inch overhang on each side of the cooker—to function as handles for lifting the finished loaf out of the cooker.
2. Process bread slices in food processor.
3. Combine breadcrumbs, beef, turkey, mushrooms, onions, Italian seasoning, salt, eggs, and garlic in bowl. Shape into loaf to fit in slow cooker.
4. Mix together ketchup, mustard, and pepper. Spread over top of loaf.
5. Cover. Cook on low 5 hours.
6. When finished, pull loaf up gently with foil handles. Place loaf on warm platter. Pull foil handles away. Allow loaf to rest for 10 minutes before slicing.

Barbecued Cola Steak

Prep time: 15 minutes | Cook time: 5½ to 6½ hours | Serves 24

1 (1.8 kg) topside or silverside steak, ¾-inch thick, cut into (3-inch) cubes
450 g ketchup

250 ml cola
115 g chopped onion
2 garlic cloves, minced
Non-stick cooking spray

1. Spray slow cooker with non-stick cooking spray.
2. Place beef pieces in cooker.
3. Mix remaining ingredients in a large bowl and pour over meat.
4. Cover and cook on high 5 to 6 hours.
5. About 30 minutes before serving, remove beef from slow cooker and shred with 2 forks. Return beef to slow cooker and mix well with sauce.
6. Cover and cook on high an additional 20 minutes.
7. Serve.

Super Beef Barbecue

Prep time: 15 minutes | Cook time: 9 to 10 hours | Serves 10 to 12

1 (1.4 to 1.8 kg) rump roast
1 clove garlic, minced, or 60 g finely chopped onion
510 g barbecue sauce

225 g ketchup
450 g pickled cucumbers, undrained

1. Cut roast into quarters and place in slow cooker.
2. In a bowl, stir together garlic, barbecue sauce, and ketchup. When well blended, fold in pickles and their juice. Pour over meat.
3. Cover and cook on low 8 to 9 hours, or until meat begins to fall apart.
4. Remove the pickles and discard them.
5. Lift the meat out onto a platter and shred by pulling it apart with 2 forks.
6. Return meat to sauce and heat thoroughly on low, about 1 hour.
7. Serve.

Yum-Yums

Prep time: 35 minutes | Cook time: 4 to 6 hours | Makes 12 sandwiches

1.4 kg minced beef
2 onions, chopped
300 g cream of chicken soup
375 ml tomato juice
1 teaspoon prepared mustard

1 teaspoon Worcestershire sauce
1 teaspoon salt
¼ teaspoon pepper

1. Brown beef and onions in skillet or frying pan. Drain.
2. Add remaining ingredients. Pour into slow cooker.
3. Cover. Cook on low 4 to 6 hours.
4. Serve.

Creamy Sloppy Joes

Prep time: 10 minutes | Cook time: 1 to 2 hours |
Makes 6 sandwiches

450 g minced beef, browned
and drained
300 g cream of mushroom soup

60 g ketchup
1 small onion, diced

1. Combine all ingredients in slow cooker.
2. Cover. Cook on low 1 to 2 hours.
3. Serve.

Mexican Goulash

Prep time: 45 minutes | Cook time: 3 to 4 hours |
Serves 8 to 10

680 to 900 g minced beef
2 onions, chopped
1 green pepper, chopped
115 g celery, chopped
1 garlic clove, minced
2 (400 g) can whole tomatoes,
cut up
1 (190 g) can tomato paste
120 g canned sliced black
olives, drained
1 (400 g) can green beans,

drained
430 g canned Mexicorn, drained
1 (400 g) can dark red kidney
beans
Diced jalapeño peppers to taste
1 teaspoon salt
¼ teaspoon pepper
1 tablespoon chilli powder
3 dashes Tabasco sauce
Shredded Cheddar cheese

1. Brown minced beef. Reserve drippings and transfer beef to slow cooker.
2. Sauté onions, pepper, celery, and garlic in drippings in skillet or frying pan. Transfer to slow cooker. Add remaining ingredients except cheese. Mix well.
3. Cover. Cook on high 3 to 4 hours.
4. Sprinkle individual servings with shredded cheese. Serve.

Tortilla Bake

Prep time: 20 minutes | Cook time: 6 to 8 hours |
Serves 6 to 8

300 g Cheddar cheese soup or
alternative such as leek and
Cheddar soup
1 (45 g) package dry taco
seasoning mix
8 corn tortillas
680 g minced beef, browned
and drained

3 medium tomatoes, coarsely
chopped
Sour cream
Shredded cheese
Spring onions, thinly sliced
Peppers, cut-up
Diced avocado
Shredded lettuce

1. Combine soup and taco seasoning.
2. Cut each tortilla into 6 wedges. Spoon one-quarter of minced beef into slow cooker. Top with one-quarter of all tortilla wedges. Spoon one-quarter of soup mixture on tortillas. Top with one-quarter of tomatoes. Repeat layers 3 times.
3. Cover. Cook on low 6 to 8 hours.
4. To serve, spoon onto plates and offer remaining ingredients as toppings.

Chinese Hamburger

Prep time: 15 minutes | Cook time: 3 to 4 hours |
Serves 8

450 g minced beef, browned
and drained
1 onion, diced
2 ribs celery, diced
300 g chicken noodle soup
300 g cream of mushroom soup
340 g Chinese vegetables

Salt to taste, about ¼ to ½
teaspoon
Pepper to taste, about ¼
teaspoon
1 green pepper, diced
1 teaspoon soy sauce

1. Combine all ingredients in slow cooker.
2. Cover. Cook on high 3 to 4 hours.
3. Serve.

Noodle Hamburger Dish

Prep time: 20 minutes | Cook time: 3 to 4 hours |
Serves 10

680 g minced beef, browned
and drained
1 green pepper, diced
950 g whole tomatoes
300 g cream of mushroom soup
1 large onion, diced

1½ tablespoons Worcestershire
sauce
225 g noodles, uncooked
1 teaspoon salt
¼ teaspoon pepper
225 g shredded cheese

1. Combine all ingredients except cheese in slow cooker.
2. Cover. Cook on high 3 to 4 hours.
3. Sprinkle with cheese before serving.

Three-Bean Burrito Bake

Prep time: 30 minutes | Cook time: 8 to 10 hours |
Serves 6

1 tablespoon oil
1 onion, chopped
1 green pepper, chopped
2 garlic cloves, minced
1 (400 g) can pinto beans,
drained
1 (400 g) can kidney beans,
drained
1 (400 g) can black beans,
drained

115 g sliced black olives,
drained
1 (113 g) can green chillies
2 (400 g) cans chopped
tomatoes
1 teaspoon chilli powder
1 teaspoon ground cumin
6 to 8 (6-inch) flour tortillas
450 g shredded Co-Jack cheese
Sour cream

1. Sauté onions, green peppers, and garlic in large skillet or frying pan in oil.
2. Add beans, olives, chillies, tomatoes, chilli powder, and cumin.
3. In greased slow cooker, layer 175 g vegetables, a tortilla, 75 g cheese. Repeat layers until all those ingredients are used, ending with sauce.
4. Cover. Cook on low 8 to 10 hours.
5. Serve with dollops of sour cream on individual servings.

Turkey-Beef Loaf

Prep time: 10 minutes | Cook time: 4 to 10 hours |
Serves 8

250 g extra-lean minced beef
450 g lean minced turkey
1 medium onion, chopped
2 eggs
150 g dry quick oats
1 envelope dry onion soup mix

(or combine onion powder with
mixed herbs)
½ to 1 teaspoon liquid smoke
1 teaspoon dry mustard
225 g ketchup, divided
Fat-free cooking spray

1.Mix beef, turkey, and chopped onion thoroughly.
2.Combine with eggs, oats, dry soup mix, liquid smoke, mustard, and all but 2 tablespoons of ketchup.
3.Shape into loaf and place in slow cooker sprayed with fat-free cooking spray. Top with remaining ketchup.
4.Cover. Cook on low 8 to 10 hours, or on high 4 to 6 hours.

Meatball-Barley Casserole

Prep time: 40 minutes | Cook time: 4 to 8 hours |
Serves 6

150 g pearl barley
450 g minced beef
115 g soft breadcrumbs
1 small onion, chopped
60 ml milk
¼ teaspoon pepper
1 teaspoon salt

Oil
115 g thinly sliced celery
115 g finely chopped sweet
peppers
300 g cream of celery soup
80 ml water
Paprika

1.Cook barley as directed on package. Set aside.
2.Combine beef, breadcrumbs, onion, milk, pepper, and salt. Shape into 20 balls. Brown on all sides in oil in skillet or frying pan. Drain and place in slow cooker.
3.Add barley, celery, and peppers.
4.Combine soup and water. Pour into slow cooker. Mix all together gently.
5.Sprinkle with paprika.
6.Cover. Cook on low 6 to 8 hours, or on high 4 hours.

Barbecue Beef on Rolls

Prep time: 10 minutes | Cook time: 6½ to 8½ hours |
Serves 12

1 (1.4 kg) boneless chuck roast
225 g barbecue sauce
115 g apricot preserve
75 g chopped green peppers

1 small onion, chopped
1 tablespoon Dijon mustard
2 teaspoons brown sugar

1.Cut roast into quarters. Place in greased slow cooker.
2.Combine barbecue sauce, preserves, green peppers, onion, mustard, and brown sugar. Pour over roast.
3.Cover. Cook on low 6 to 8 hours. Remove roast and slice thinly. Return to slow cooker. Stir gently.
4.Cover. Cook 20 to 30 minutes.
5.Serve.

Cheeseburger Casserole

Prep time: 20 minutes | Cook time: 3 hours | Serves 6

450 g minced beef
1 small onion, chopped
1 teaspoon salt
Dash of pepper
115 g breadcrumbs

1 egg
Tomato juice to moisten
1.1 kg mashed potatoes
9 slices processed cheese

1.Combine beef, onions, salt, pepper, breadcrumbs, egg, and tomato juice. Place one-third of mixture in slow cooker.
2.Spread with one-third of mashed potatoes and 3 slices cheese. Repeat 2 times.
3.Cover. Cook on low 3 hours.

Stuffed "Baked" Topping

Prep time: 35 minutes | Cook time: 1 hour | Serves 12

1.4 kg minced beef
225 g chopped green peppers
115 g chopped onions
6 tablespoons butter
60 g flour
750 ml milk
115 g pimento or chopped
sweet red peppers

340 g Cheddar cheese
340 g your favourite mild
cheese
½ teaspoon hot pepper sauce
¼ teaspoon dry mustard
Salt to taste
12 baked potatoes

1.Brown minced beef, green peppers, and onions in butter. Transfer mixture to slow cooker, reserving drippings.
2.Stir flour into drippings. Slowly add milk. Cook until thickened.
3.Add pimento, cheeses, and seasonings. Pour over ingredients in slow cooker.
4.Cover. Heat on low.
5.Serve over baked potatoes, each one split open on an individual dinner plate.

Gourmet Meat Loaf

Prep time: 25 minutes | Cook time: 8 to 12 hours |
Serves 8

2 medium potatoes, cut in strips
Meat loaf:
900 g minced beef
250 g sausage meat
1 onion, finely chopped
2 to 3 cloves garlic, minced,
according to your taste
preference
115 g ketchup
175 g crushed salt crackers

2 eggs
2 teaspoons Worcestershire
sauce
2 teaspoons seasoned salt
¼ teaspoon pepper
Sauce:
115 g ketchup
60 g brown sugar
1½ teaspoons dry mustard
½ teaspoon ground nutmeg

1.Place potatoes in bottom of slow cooker.
2.Combine meat loaf ingredients. Form into loaf and place on top of potatoes.
3.Combine sauce ingredients. Spoon over meat loaf.
4.Cover. Cook on low 8 to 12 hours.

Unforgettable Sloppy Joes

Prep time: 10 minutes | Cook time: 4 to 5 hours |
Makes 4 to 6 sandwiches

450 g minced beef
1 onion, chopped
175 g ketchup
2 tablespoons chilli sauce
1 tablespoon Worcestershire

sauce
1 tablespoon prepared mustard
1 tablespoon vinegar
1 tablespoon sugar

1.Brown beef and onion in saucepan. Drain.
2.Combine all ingredients in slow cooker.
3.Cover. Cook on low 4 to 5 hours.
4.Serve

Barbecued Hamburgers

Prep time: 20 minutes | Cook time: 3 to 6 hours |
Makes 4 sandwiches

450 g minced beef
60 g chopped onions
3 tablespoons ketchup
1 teaspoon salt

1 egg, beaten
60 g seasoned breadcrumbs
510 g of your favourite
barbecue sauce

1.Combine beef, onions, ketchup, salt, egg, and breadcrumbs. Form into 4 patties. Brown both sides lightly in skillet or frying pan. Place in slow cooker.
2.Cover with barbecue sauce.
3.Cover. Cook on high 3 hours, or on low 6 hours.

Pizzaburgers

Prep time: 20 minutes | Cook time: 1 to 2 hours |
Makes 4 to 6 sandwiches

450 g minced beef
115 g chopped onions
¼ teaspoon salt
⅛ teaspoon pepper

250 g pizza sauce
300 g cream of mushroom soup
450 g shredded Cheddar cheese

1.Brown minced beef and onion in skillet or frying pan. Drain.
2.Add remaining ingredients. Mix well. Pour into slow cooker.
3.Cover. Cook on low 1 to 2 hours.
4.Serve.

Beef Roast Barbecue Sandwiches

Prep time: 10 minutes | Cook time: 10 to 12 hours |
Makes 10 to 12 sandwiches

1.4 to 1.8 kg beef roast (bottom round or rump is best)
250 ml water, divided
115 g ketchup
1 teaspoon chilli powder
1½ tablespoons Worcestershire

sauce
2 tablespoons vinegar
1 teaspoon salt
1 tablespoon sugar
1 teaspoon dry mustard
1 medium onion, finely chopped

1.The night before serving, place roast in slow cooker with 125 ml water.
2.Cover. Cook on low 10 to 12 hours.
3.Also, the night before serving, combine remaining ingredients and refrigerate 8 to 10 hours.
4.In the morning, shred roast with fork and return to cooker. Pour remaining ingredients over top. Mix together.
5.Heat on low until mealtime.
6.Serve.

Savoury Sloppy Joes

Prep time: 30 minutes | Cook time: 2 to 3 hours |
Makes 8 to 10 sandwiches

900 g minced beef
1 onion, finely chopped
115 g ketchup
1 teaspoon salt (optional)

1 teaspoon Worcestershire
sauce
300 g cream of mushroom soup

1.Brown minced beef and onion together in non-stick skillet or frying pan. Drain.
2.Place in slow cooker. Stir in remaining ingredients.
3.Cook on high for 2 to 3 hours, or until heated through.
4.Serve.

Granny's Delight

Prep time: 20 minutes | Cook time: 1½ hours |
Serves 5

450 g minced beef
1 small onion, chopped
675 g dry macaroni
225 g shredded Cheddar cheese
900 g spaghetti or pasta sauce,

your favourite packaged or
homemade
125 ml water
Non-stick cooking spray

1.Brown beef with chopped onion in a non-stick skillet or frying pan. Drain.
2.Spray interior of slow cooker with non-stick cooking spray. Place all ingredients into slow cooker and fold together gently.
3.Cover and cook on high for 1½ hours, or until macaroni is tender but not mushy.

Low-Fat Slow Cooker Barbecue

Prep time: 20 minutes | Cook time: 4 hours | Serves 12

450 g extra-lean minced beef
450 g celery, chopped fine
225 g onions, chopped
1 tablespoon whipped butter
2 tablespoons red wine vinegar
1 tablespoon brown sugar

3 tablespoons Worcestershire
sauce
1 teaspoon salt
1 teaspoon English mustard
225 g ketchup
500 ml water

1.Brown minced beef, celery, and onions in a non-stick skillet or frying pan.
2.Combine all ingredients in slow cooker.
3.Cover and cook on high for 4 hours.
4.Serve.

Ranch Hand Beef

Prep time: 10 minutes | Cook time: 4 to 9 hours |
Serves 10 to 12

1 (1.4 to 1.6 kg) boneless beef chuck roast
225 g thinly sliced onions
300 g cream of celery soup
115 g canned sliced mushrooms
1 (330 ml) can beer
115 g ketchup

1 large bay leaf
½ teaspoon salt
¼ teaspoon lemon pepper
2 tablespoons chopped fresh parsley, or 1½ teaspoons dried parsley

1. Place roast in slow cooker.
2. Combine remaining ingredients. Pour over roast.
3. Cover. Cook on low 7 to 9 hours or on Medium setting 4 to 6 hours, until meat is tender.
4. Remove bay leaf.
5. Shred roast with two forks. Mix meat through sauce.
6. Serve.

Easy Roast Beef Barbecue

Prep time: 10 minutes | Cook time: 12 hours |
Serves 12 to 16

1 (1.4 to 1.8 kg) beef roasting joint
340 g bottle barbecue sauce
125 ml water

115 g ketchup
115 g chopped onions
115 g chopped green pepper

1. Combine ingredients in slow cooker.
2. Cover. Cook on low 12 hours.
3. Shred meat using 2 forks. Mix thoroughly through sauce.
4. Serve.

Barbecued Spoonburgers

Prep time: 15 minutes | Cook time: 3 to 8 hours |
Serves 6 to 8

2 tablespoons oil
680 g minced beef
115 g chopped onions
115 g diced celery
Half a green pepper, chopped
1 tablespoon Worcestershire sauce
115 g ketchup
1 garlic clove, minced

1 teaspoon salt
175 ml water
⅛ teaspoon pepper
½ teaspoon paprika
1 (190 g) tube tomato paste
2 tablespoons vinegar
2 teaspoons brown sugar
1 teaspoon dry mustard

1. Brown beef in oil in saucepan. Drain.
2. Combine all ingredients in slow cooker.
3. Cover. Cook on low 6 to 8 hours, or on high 3 to 4 hours.
4. Serve.

Potluck Beef Barbecue

Prep time: 10 minutes | Cook time: 6½ to 8¾ hours |
Serves 16

1 (1.8 kg) beef chuck roast
250 ml brewed coffee or water
1 tablespoon cider or red-wine vinegar
1 teaspoon salt
½ teaspoon pepper

400 g ketchup
425 g tomato sauce
250 g sweet pickle relish
2 tablespoons Worcestershire sauce
60 g brown sugar

1. Place roast, coffee, vinegar, salt, and pepper in slow cooker.
2. Cover. Cook on high 6 to 8 hours, or until meat is very tender.
3. Pour off cooking liquid. Shred meat with two forks.
4. Add remaining ingredients. Stir well.
5. Cover. Cook on high 30 to 45 minutes. Reduce heat to low for serving.

Minced beef Pizza Fondue

Prep time: 10 minutes | Cook time: 2 to 3 hours |
Serves 8 to 12

450 g minced beef
400 g pizza sauce with cheese or regular pizza sauce
250 g Cheddar cheese, shredded
250 g Mozzarella cheese,

shredded
1 teaspoon dried oregano
½ teaspoon fennel seed (optional)
1 tablespoon cornflour

1. Brown beef, crumble fine, and drain.
2. Combine all ingredients in slow cooker.
3. Cover. Heat on low 2 to 3 hours.
4. Serve.

Stuffed Peppers with Beef

Prep time: 15 minutes | Cook time: 4 to 12 hours |
Serves 6 to 8

6 to 8 green peppers
450 to 900 g minced beef
1 onion, chopped
¼ teaspoon salt
¼ teaspoon pepper

1 egg
1 slice white bread
2 (400 g) can whole or stewed tomatoes

1. Cut peppers in half and remove seeds.
2. Combine minced beef, onion, salt, pepper, and egg. Tear bread into small pieces. Add to minced beef mixture. Stuff into peppers.
3. Form remaining meat into oblong shape. Place meatloaf and peppers into slow cooker. Pour in tomatoes.
4. Cover. Cook on low 6 to 12 hours, or on high 4 to 5 hours.

Chapter 5 Poultry

Pacific Chicken

Prep time: 10 minutes | Cook time: 7 to 8 hours |
Serves 6

6 to 8 skinless chicken thighs	2 tablespoons grated fresh
120 ml soy sauce	ginger
2 tablespoons brown sugar	2 garlic cloves, minced

1. Wash and dry chicken. Place in slow cooker.
2. Combine remaining ingredients. Pour over chicken.
3. Cover. Cook on high 1 hour. Reduce heat to low and cook 6 to 7 hours.
4. Serve.

Thai Chicken

Prep time: 5 minutes | Cook time: 8 to 9 hours |
Serves 6

6 skinless chicken thighs	1 teaspoon grated fresh ginger
200 g salsa, your choice of heat	(optional)
60 g chunky peanut butter	2 tablespoons chopped
1 tablespoon low-sodium soy	coriander (optional)
sauce	1 tablespoon chopped dry-
2 tablespoons lime juice	roasted peanuts (optional)

1. Put chicken in slow cooker.
2. In a bowl, mix remaining ingredients together, except coriander and chopped peanuts.
3. Cover and cook on low 8 to 9 hours, or until chicken is cooked through but not dry.
4. Skim off any fat. Remove chicken to a platter and serve topped with sauce. Sprinkle with peanuts and coriander, if you wish.
5. Serve.

Chicken and Apples

Prep time: 20 minutes | Cook time: 7 to 8 hours |
Serves 6

180 ml orange juice concentrate	6 skinless, boneless chicken
½ teaspoon dried marjoram	breast halves
leaves	3 Granny Smith apples, cored
Dash ground nutmeg	and sliced
Dash garlic powder	60 ml water
1 onion, chopped	2 tablespoons corn flour

1. In a small bowl, combine orange juice concentrate, marjoram, nutmeg, and garlic powder.
2. Place onions in bottom of slow cooker.

3. Dip each chicken breast into the orange mixture to coat. Then place in slow cooker over onions.
4. Pour any remaining orange juice concentrate mixture over the chicken.
5. Cover. Cook on low 6 to 7 hours.
6. Add apples and cook on low 1 hour longer.
7. Remove chicken, apples, and onions to a serving platter.
8. Pour the sauce that remains into a medium saucepan.
9. Mix together water and corn flour. Stir into the juices.
10. Cook over medium heat, stirring constantly until the sauce is thick and bubbly.
11. Serve the sauce over the chicken.

Cranberry Chicken

Prep time: 10 minutes | Cook time: 6 to 8 hours |
Serves 6

6 chicken breast halves, divided	1 envelope dry onion soup mix
1 (227 g) bottle Catalina or	1 (454 g) can whole cranberry
Creamy French salad dressing	sauce

1. Place 3 chicken breasts in slow cooker.
2. Mix other ingredients together in a mixing bowl. Pour half the sauce over chicken in the cooker.
3. Repeat Steps 1 and 2.
4. Cover and cook on low 6 to 8 hours, or until chicken is tender but not dry.

Chicken Enchilada Casserole

Prep time: 30 minutes | Cook time: 6 to 8 hours |
Serves 4 to 6

1 onion, chopped	3 boneless chicken breast
1 garlic clove, minced	halves, cooked and cubed
1 tablespoon oil	1 (425 g) can ranch-style beans,
1 (283 g) can enchilada sauce	drained
1 (227 g) can tomato sauce	1 (312 g) can Mexicorn, drained
Salt to taste	340 g Cheddar cheese, shredded
Pepper to taste	65 g sliced black olives, drained
8 corn tortillas	

1. Sauté onion and garlic in oil in saucepan. Stir in enchilada sauce and tomato sauce. Season with salt and pepper.
2. Place two tortillas in bottom of slow cooker. Layer one-third chicken on top. Top with one-third sauce mixture, one-third beans, one-third corn, one-third cheese, and one-third black olives. Repeat layers 2 more times. Top with 2 tortillas.
3. Cover. Cook on low 6 to 8 hours.

Herby Barbecued Chicken

Prep time: 10 minutes | Cook time: 6 to 8 hours |
Serves 4 to 6

1 whole chicken, cut up, or 8 of your favorite pieces	Barbecue Sauce
1 onion, thinly sliced	1 teaspoon dried oregano
1 bottle Sweet Baby Ray's	1 teaspoon dried basil

1. Place chicken in slow cooker.
2. Mix onion slices, sauce, oregano, and basil together in a bowl. Pour over chicken, covering as well as possible.
3. Cover and cook on low 6 to 8 hours, or until chicken is tender but not dry.

Come-Back-for-More Barbecued Chicken

Prep time: 10 minutes | Cook time: 6 to 8 hours |
Serves 6 to 8

6 to 8 chicken breast halves	105 g brown sugar
235 g ketchup	1 teaspoon chili powder
80 ml Worcestershire sauce	120 ml water

1. Place chicken in slow cooker.
2. Whisk remaining ingredients in a large bowl. Pour sauce mixture over chicken.
3. Cover and cook on low 6 to 8 hours, or until chicken is tender but not overcooked.

Easy Chicken

Prep time: 10 minutes | Cook time: 8 hours | Serves
6 to 8

8 to 10 chicken wings or legs and thighs	100 g sugar
120 ml soy sauce	½ teaspoon Tabasco sauce
	Pinch of ground ginger

1. Place chicken in greased slow cooker.
2. Combine remaining ingredients and pour over chicken.
3. Cover. Cook on low 8 hours.
4. Serve.

Cranberry Barbecued Chicken

Prep time: 10 minutes | Cook time: 4 to 8 hours |
Serves 6 to 8

1.4 to 1.8 kg chicken pieces	80 g diced onions
½ teaspoon salt	1 (454 g) can whole-berry cranberry sauce
¼ teaspoon pepper	
50 g diced celery	280 g barbecue sauce

1. Combine all ingredients in slow cooker.
2. Cover. Cook on high for 4 hours, or on low 6 to 8 hours.

Barbecued Chicken Breasts

Prep time: 10 minutes | Cook time: 3 to 8 hours |
Serves 8

8 boneless, skinless chicken breast halves	sauce
	60 ml cider vinegar
1 (227 g) can low-sodium tomato sauce	½ teaspoon salt
	¼ teaspoon black pepper
240 ml water	Dash of garlic powder
2 tablespoons brown sugar	Dash of dried oregano
2 tablespoons prepared mustard	3 tablespoons onion, chopped
2 tablespoons Worcestershire	Nonfat cooking spray

1. Place chicken in slow cooker sprayed with nonfat cooking spray. Overlap chicken as little as possible.
2. Combine remaining ingredients. Pour over chicken.
3. Cover. Cook on low 6 to 8 hours, or on high 3 to 4 hours.
4. To thicken the sauce a bit, remove the lid during the last hour of cooking.

Chicken and Potatoes Barbecue

Prep time: 10 minutes | Cook time: 4 to 9 hours |
Serves 8

8 boneless, skinless chicken breast halves, divided	280 g honey barbecue sauce
	1 (454 g) can jellied cranberry sauce
8 small or medium potatoes, quartered, divided	
	Nonfat cooking spray

1. Spray slow cooker with nonstick cooking spray. Place 4 chicken breasts in slow cooker.
2. Top with 4 cut-up potatoes.
3. Mix barbecue sauce and cranberry sauce together in a bowl. Spoon half the sauce over the chicken and potatoes in the cooker.
4. Place remaining breasts in cooker, followed by the remaining potato chunks. Pour rest of sauce over all.
5. Cover and cook on low 8 to 9 hours, or on high 4 hours, or until chicken and potatoes are tender but not dry.

Chicken with Applesauce

Prep time: 20 minutes | Cook time: 2 to 3 hours |
Serves 4

4 boneless, skinless chicken breast halves	500 g applesauce
	70 g barbecue sauce
Salt to taste	½ teaspoon poultry seasoning
Pepper to taste	2 teaspoons honey
4 to 5 tablespoons oil	½ teaspoon lemon juice

1. Season chicken with salt and pepper. Brown in oil for 5 minutes per side.
2. Cut up chicken into 1-inch chunks and transfer to slow cooker.
3. Combine remaining ingredients. Pour over chicken and mix together well.
4. Cover. Cook on high 2 to 3 hours, or until chicken is tender.
5. Serve.

Coq au Vin

Prep time: 25 minutes | Cook time: 5 to 6 hours | Serves 6

4 slices turkey bacon
205 g frozen pearl onions
95 g fresh, sliced, button mushrooms
1 clove garlic, minced
1 teaspoon dried thyme leaves
¼ teaspoon coarse ground black pepper

6 boneless, skinless chicken breast halves
120 ml dry red wine
180 ml fat-free, low-sodium chicken broth
6 g tomato paste
3 tablespoons plain flour

1. Cook bacon in medium frying pan over medium heat. Drain and crumble.
2. Layer ingredients in slow cooker in the following order: onions, crumbled bacon, mushrooms, garlic, thyme, pepper, chicken, wine, and broth.
3. Cover. Cook on low 5 to 6 hours.
4. Remove chicken and vegetables. Cover. Keep warm.
5. Ladle 120 ml cooking liquid into small bowl. Allow to cool slightly.
6. Turn slow cooker to high. Cover.
7. Mix removed liquid, tomato paste, and flour until smooth.
8. Return tomato mixture to slow cooker.
9. Cover. Cook 15 minutes or until thickened.
10. Serve.

Chicken Alfredo

Prep time: 20 minutes | Cook time: 8 hours | Serves 4 to 6

1 (454 g) jar Alfredo sauce
4 to 6 boneless, skinless chicken breast halves
230 g dry noodles, cooked
1 (113 g) can mushroom pieces

and stems, drained
115 g shredded Mozzarella cheese, or 75 g grated Parmesan cheese

1. Pour about one-third of Alfredo sauce in bottom of slow cooker.
2. Add chicken and cover with remaining sauce.
3. Cover. Cook on low 8 hours.
4. Fifteen minutes before serving, add noodles and mushrooms, mixing well. Sprinkle top with cheese. Dish is ready to serve when cheese is melted.
5. Serve.

Chicken in a Hurry

Prep time: 10 minutes | Cook time: 4 to 8 hours | Serves 4 to 5

1.1 to 1.4 kg skinless chicken drumsticks
120 g ketchup

60 ml water
50 g brown sugar
1 package dry onion soup mix

1. Arrange chicken in slow cooker.
2. Combine remaining ingredients. Pour over chicken.
3. Cover. Cook on high 4 to 5 hours, or on low 7 to 8 hours.

Turkey Meat Loaf

Prep time: 15 minutes | Cook time: 6 to 8 hours | Serves 8

680 g lean minced turkey
2 egg whites
80 g ketchup
1 tablespoon Worcestershire sauce
1 teaspoon dried basil

½ teaspoon salt
½ teaspoon black pepper
2 small onions, chopped
2 potatoes, finely shredded
2 small red bell peppers, finely chopped

1. Combine all ingredients in a large bowl.
2. Shape into a loaf to fit in your slow cooker. Place in slow cooker.
3. Cover. Cook on low 6 to 8 hours.

Savory Turkey Meatballs in Italian Sauce

Prep time: 30 minutes | Cook time: 6 to 8 hours | Serves 8

1 (794 g) can crushed tomatoes
1 tablespoon red wine vinegar
1 medium onion, finely chopped
2 garlic cloves, minced
¼ teaspoon Italian herb seasoning
1 teaspoon dried basil
455 g minced turkey
⅛ teaspoon garlic powder

⅛ teaspoon black pepper
6 g dried parsley
2 egg whites
¼ teaspoon dried minced onion
30 g quick oats
40 g grated Parmesan cheese
30 g plain flour
Oil

1. Combine tomatoes, vinegar, onions, garlic, Italian seasonings, and basil in slow cooker. Turn to low.
2. Combine remaining ingredients, except flour and oil. Form into 1-inch balls. Dredge each ball in flour. Brown in oil in a frying pan over medium heat. Transfer to slow cooker. Stir into sauce.
3. Cover. Cook on low 6 to 8 hours.
4. Serve.

Saucy Turkey Meatballs

Prep time: 20 minutes | Cook time: 6 to 8 hours | Serves 6

230 g lean minced turkey
95 g oat bran
1 clove garlic, crushed
2 tablespoons water
1 tablespoon low-sodium soy sauce

3 egg whites
80 g onions, diced
140 g low-sodium chili sauce
145 g grape jelly
65 g Dijon mustard

1. Combine turkey, oat bran, garlic, water, soy sauce, egg whites, and onions. Shape into 24 balls (1 tablespoon per ball).
2. Place meatballs on baking sheet and bake at 176°C for 15 to 20 minutes until browned. (They can be made ahead and frozen.)
3. Mix together chili sauce, grape jelly, and Dijon mustard.
4. Combine meatballs and sauce in slow cooker.
5. Cover. Cook on low 6 to 8 hours.

Gran's Big Potluck

Prep time: 20 minutes | Cook time: 10 to 12 hours | Serves 10 to 15

1.1 to 1.4 kg stewing hen, cut into pieces
230 g stewing beef, cubed
230 g veal shoulder or roast, cubed
1.4 litres water
230 g small red potatoes, cubed
230 g small onions, cut in half
150 g sliced carrots
100 g chopped celery
1 green pepper, chopped

455 g frozen lima beans
100 g fresh or frozen okra
165 g whole-kernel corn
1 (227 g) can whole tomatoes with juice
1 (425 g) can tomato puree
1 teaspoon salt
¼ to ½ teaspoon pepper
1 teaspoon dry mustard
½ teaspoon chili powder
4 g chopped fresh parsley

1. Combine all ingredients except last 5 seasonings in one very large slow cooker, or divide between two medium-sized ones.
2. Cover. Cook on low 10 to 12 hours. Add seasonings during last hour of cooking.

Chicken and Seafood Gumbo

Prep time: 45 minutes | Cook time: 10 to 12 hours | Serves 12

100 g chopped celery
160 g chopped onions
75 g chopped green peppers
60 ml olive oil
30 g, plus 1 tablespoon, plain flour
1.4 litres chicken stock
900 g chicken, cut up

3 bay leaves
150 g sliced okra
1 (340 g) can diced tomatoes
1 teaspoon Tabasco sauce
Salt to taste
Pepper to taste
455 g ready-to-eat prawns
8 g snipped fresh parsley

1. Sauté celery, onions, and peppers in oil. Blend in flour and chicken stock until smooth. Cook 5 minutes. Pour into slow cooker.
2. Add remaining ingredients except seafood and parsley.
3. Cover. Cook on low 10 to 12 hours.
4. One hour before serving add prawns and parsley.
5. Remove bay leaves before serving.
6. Serve.

Chili Barbecued Chicken Wings

Prep time: 5 minutes | Cook time: 2 to 8 hours | Serves 10

2.3 kg chicken wings, tips cut off
1 (340 g) bottle chili sauce
80 ml lemon juice
1 tablespoon Worcestershire sauce

2 tablespoons molasses
1 teaspoon salt
2 teaspoons chili powder
¼ teaspoon hot pepper sauce
Dash garlic powder

1. Place wings in cooker.
2. Combine remaining ingredients and pour over chicken.
3. Cover. Cook on low 6 to 8 hours, or on high 2 to 3 hours.

Loretta's Hot Chicken

Prep time: 15 minutes | Cook time: 2 hours | Serves 12

1.1 kg cubed cooked chicken or turkey
1 medium onion, chopped

100 g chopped celery
460 g mayonnaise
125 g cubed American cheese

1. Combine all ingredients except buns in slow cooker.
2. Cover. Cook on high 2 hours.
3. Serve.

Barbecue Chicken for Buns

Prep time: 15 minutes | Cook time: 8 hours | Serves 16 to 20

840 g diced cooked chicken
200 g chopped celery
160 g chopped onions
150 g chopped green peppers
4 tablespoons butter
470 g ketchup

480 ml water
2 tablespoons brown sugar
4 tablespoons vinegar
2 teaspoons dry mustard
1 teaspoon pepper
1 teaspoon salt

1. Combine all ingredients in slow cooker.
2. Cover. Cook on low 8 hours.
3. Stir chicken until it shreds.
4. Serve.

Marinated Chinese Chicken Salad

Prep time: 25 minutes | Cook time: 3 to 8 hours | Serves 8

Marinade:
3 cloves minced garlic
1 tablespoon fresh ginger, grated
1 teaspoon dried red pepper flakes
2 tablespoons honey
3 tablespoons low-sodium soy sauce
6 boneless, skinless chicken breast halves
Dressing:

120 ml rice wine vinegar
1 clove garlic, minced
1 teaspoon fresh grated ginger
1 tablespoon honey
Salad:
1 large head iceberg lettuce, shredded
2 carrots, julienned
75 g chopped roasted peanuts
4 g chopped coriander
½ package dried noodles, fried in hot oil

1. Mix marinade ingredients in a small bowl.
2. Place chicken in slow cooker and pour marinade over chicken, coating each piece well.
3. Cover. Cook on low 6 to 8 hours, or on high 3 to 4 hours.
4. Remove chicken from slow cooker and cool. Reserve juices. Shred chicken into bite-sized pieces.
5. In a small bowl, combine the dressing ingredients with 120 ml of the juice from the slow cooker.
6. In a large serving bowl toss together the shredded chicken, lettuce, carrots, peanuts, coriander, and noodles.
7. Just before serving, drizzle with the salad dressing. Toss well and serve.

Chicken Gumbo

Prep time: 25 minutes | Cook time: 3 to 10 hours |

Serves 6 to 8

1 large onion, chopped
3 to 4 garlic cloves, minced
1 green pepper, diced
200 g okra, sliced
360 g tomatoes, chopped

960 ml chicken broth
455 g chicken breast, cut into
1-inch pieces
2 teaspoons Old Bay Seasoning

1. Combine all ingredients in slow cooker.
2. Cover. Cook on low 8 to 10 hours, or on high 3 to 4 hours.
3. Serve.

Lemon Chicken

Prep time: 20 minutes | Cook time: 3½ to 4½ hours |

Serves 6

6 boneless, skinless chicken
breast halves
1 teaspoon dried oregano
½ teaspoon seasoned salt
¼ teaspoon black pepper
60 ml water

3 tablespoons lemon juice
2 garlic cloves, minced
2 teaspoons chicken bouillon
granules
2 teaspoons fresh parsley,
minced

1. Pat chicken dry with paper towels.
2. Combine oregano, seasoned salt, and pepper. Rub over chicken.
3. Brown chicken in a nonstick frying pan over medium heat.
4. Place chicken in slow cooker.
5. Combine water, lemon juice, garlic, and bouillon in a frying pan. Bring to a boil, stirring to loosen browned bits. Pour over chicken.
6. Cover. Cook on low 3 to 4 hours.
7. Baste chicken. Add parsley.
8. Remove lid and cook 15 to 30 minutes longer, allowing juices to thicken slightly.
9. Serve.

Chicken and Sun-Dried Tomatoes

Prep time: 20 minutes | Cook time: 4 to 6 hours |

Serves 8

1 tablespoon olive oil
1.4 kg boneless, skinless
chicken breasts, cut in 8 serving
pieces
2 garlic cloves, minced
120 ml white wine

360 ml fat-free, low-sodium
chicken stock
1 teaspoon dried basil
30 g chopped, sun-dried
tomatoes, cut into slivers

1. Heat oil in a frying pan. Add several pieces of chicken at a time, but make sure not to crowd the frying pan so the chicken can brown evenly.
2. Transfer chicken to slow cooker as it finishes browning.
3. Add garlic, wine, chicken stock, and basil to frying pan. Bring to a boil. Scrape up any bits from the bottom of the pan.
4. Pour over chicken. Scatter tomatoes over the top.
5. Cover. Cook on low 4 to 6 hours.

Southern Barbecue Spaghetti Sauce

Prep time: 20 minutes | Cook time: 4 to 5 hours |

Serves 12

455 g lean minced turkey
2 medium onions, chopped
115 g sliced fresh mushrooms
1 medium green bell pepper,
chopped
2 garlic cloves, minced
1 (411 g) can diced tomatoes,
undrained
1 (340 g) can tomato paste

1 (227 g) can tomato sauce
235 g ketchup
120 ml fat-free beef broth
2 tablespoons Worcestershire
sauce
2 tablespoons brown sugar
1 tablespoon ground cumin
2 teaspoons chili powder
1.2 kg spaghetti, cooked

1. In a large nonstick frying pan, cook the turkey, onions, mushrooms, green pepper, and garlic over medium heat until meat is no longer pink. Drain.
2. Transfer to slow cooker. Stir in tomatoes, tomato paste, tomato sauce, ketchup, broth, Worcestershire sauce, brown sugar, cumin, and chili powder. Mix well.
3. Cook on low 4 to 5 hours. Serve over spaghetti.

Noodleless Lasagna

Prep time: 20 minutes | Cook time: 4 to 4½ hours |

Serves 4

680 g fat-free minced turkey
340 g meat-free, low-sodium
spaghetti sauce
230 g sliced mushrooms
375 g fat-free ricotta cheese
1 egg, beaten

115 g shredded Mozzarella
cheese (part skim), divided
1½ teaspoons Italian seasoning
10 slices turkey pepperoni
Nonfat cooking spray

1. Brown minced turkey in a nonstick frying pan.
2. Add spaghetti sauce and mushrooms and mix with meat.
3. Pour half of turkey mixture into slow cooker sprayed with nonfat cooking spray.
4. In a small bowl, mix together the ricotta cheese, egg, 60 g of Mozzarella, and the Italian seasoning. Beat well with a fork.
5. Lay half of pepperoni slices on top of turkey mixture.
6. Spread half of cheese mixture over pepperoni.
7. Repeat layers, finishing by sprinkling the remaining Mozzarella on top.
8. Cover. Cook on low 4 to 4½ hours.

Cabbage Joe

Prep time: 10 minutes | Cook time: 6 to 9 hours |

Serves 6

455 g lean minced turkey
270 g shredded cabbage

560 g barbecue sauce

1. Brown turkey in a nonstick frying pan over medium heat.
2. Combine cabbage, turkey, and sauce in slow cooker.
3. Cover. Cook on low 6 to 8 hours.

Chicken at a Whim

Prep time: 10 minutes | Cook time: 4½ hours | Serves 6 to 8

6 medium, boneless, skinless chicken breast halves
1 small onion, sliced
240 ml dry white wine, chicken broth, or water
1 (425 g) can chicken broth
480 ml water
1 (170 g) can sliced black

olives, with juice
1 small can artichoke hearts, with juice
5 garlic cloves, minced
125 g dry elbow macaroni or small shells
1 envelope dry savory garlic soup

1. Place chicken in slow cooker. Spread onion over chicken.
2. Combine remaining ingredients, except dry soup mix, and pour over chicken. Sprinkle with dry soup.
3. Cover. Cook on low 4½ hours.

Pumpkin Black Bean Turkey Chili

Prep time: 20 minutes | Cook time: 7 to 8 hours | Serves 10 to 12

160 g chopped onions
150 g chopped yellow bell pepper
3 garlic cloves, minced
2 tablespoons oil
1½ teaspoons dried oregano
1½ to 2 teaspoons ground cumin

2 teaspoons chili powder
2 (425 g) cans black beans, rinsed and drained
350 g cooked turkey, chopped
1 (454 g) can pumpkin
1 (411 g) can diced tomatoes
720 ml chicken broth

1. Sauté onions, yellow pepper, and garlic in oil for 8 minutes, or until soft.
2. Stir in oregano, cumin, and chili powder.
3. Cook 1 minute. Transfer to slow cooker. Add remaining ingredients.
4. Cover. Cook on low 7 to 8 hours.

Chicken and Prawn Casserole

Prep time: 20 minutes | Cook time: 3 to 8 hours | Serves 6

265 g rice, uncooked
2 tablespoons butter, melted
720 ml fat-free, low-sodium chicken broth
240 ml water
420 g cut-up, cooked skinless chicken breast

2 (113 g) cans sliced mushrooms, drained
80 ml light soy sauce
340 g shelled frozen prawns
8 spring onions, chopped, 2 tablespoons reserved
60 g slivered almonds

1. Combine rice and butter in slow cooker. Stir to coat rice well.
2. Add remaining ingredients except almonds and 2 tablespoons spring onions.
3. Cover. Cook on low 6 to 8 hours, or on high 3 to 4 hours, until rice is tender.
4. Sprinkle almonds and spring onions over top before serving.

Creamy Italian Chicken

Prep time: 10 minutes | Cook time: 4 hours | Serves 4

4 boneless, skinless chicken breast halves
1 envelope dry Italian salad dressing mix
60 ml water

225 g cream cheese, softened
1 (305 g) can cream of chicken or celery soup
1 (113 g) can mushroom stems and pieces, drained (optional)

1. Place chicken in slow cooker. Combine salad dressing and water. Pour over chicken.
2. Cover and cook on low 3 hours.
3. In a small bowl, beat cream cheese and soup until blended. Stir in mushrooms if you wish. Pour over chicken.
4. Cover and cook on low 1 hour, or until chicken is tender but not dry.

Chicken and Sausage Cacciatore

Prep time: 35 minutes | Cook time: 8 hours | Serves 4 to 6

1 large green pepper, sliced in 1-inch strips
75 g sliced mushrooms
1 medium onion, sliced in rings
455 g skinless, boneless chicken breasts, browned

455 g Italian-style sausage, browned
½ teaspoon dried oregano
½ teaspoon dried basil
340 g Italian-style tomato sauce

1. Layer vegetables in slow cooker.
2. Top with meat.
3. Sprinkle with oregano and basil.
4. Top with tomato sauce.
5. Cover. Cook on low 8 hours.
6. Remove cover during last 30 minutes of cooking time to allow sauce to cook off and thicken.
7. Serve.

Zesty Chicken Breasts

Prep time: 15 minutes | Cook time: 3 to 8 hours | Serves 6

6 bone-in chicken breast halves
2 (411 g) cans diced tomatoes, undrained
1 small can jalapeños, sliced and drained (optional)

60 g reduced-fat, creamy peanut butter
2 tablespoons fresh coriander, chopped (optional)
Nonfat cooking spray

1. Remove skin from chicken, but leave bone in.
2. Mix all ingredients, except chicken, in medium-sized bowl.
3. Pour one-third of sauce in bottom of slow cooker sprayed with nonfat cooking spray. Place chicken on top.
4. Pour remaining sauce over chicken.
5. Cover. Cook on high 3 to 4 hours, or on low 6 to 8 hours.
6. Remove from slow cooker gently. Chicken will be very tender and will fall off the bones.

Turkey with Mushroom Sauce

Prep time: 15 minutes | Cook time: 7 to 8 hours |
Serves 12

1 large boneless, skinless turkey breast, halved	¼ teaspoon black pepper
2 tablespoons butter, melted	120 ml white wine
2 tablespoons dried parsley	75 g sliced fresh mushrooms
½ teaspoon dried oregano	2 tablespoons corn flour
½ teaspoon salt	60 ml cold water

1. Place turkey in slow cooker. Brush with butter.
2. Mix together parsley, oregano, salt, pepper, and wine. Pour over turkey.
3. Top with mushrooms.
4. Cover. Cook on low 7 to 8 hours.
5. Remove turkey and keep warm.
6. Skim any fat from cooking juices.
7. In a saucepan, combine corn flour and water until smooth. Gradually add cooking juices. Bring to a boil. Cook and stir 2 minutes until thickened.
8. Slice turkey and serve with sauce.

Slow-Cooked Turkey Dinner

Prep time: 15 minutes | Cook time: 7½ hours |
Serves 4 to 6

1 onion, diced	2 tablespoons dry onion soup mix
6 small red potatoes, quartered	1 (305 g) can cream of mushroom soup
300 g sliced carrots	160 ml chicken broth or water
680 to 900 g boneless, skinless turkey thighs	
30 g plain flour	

1. Place vegetables in bottom of slow cooker.
2. Place turkey thighs over vegetables.
3. Combine remaining ingredients. Pour over turkey.
4. Cover. Cook on high 30 minutes. Reduce heat to low and cook 7 hours.

Barbecued Turkey Legs

Prep time: 10 minutes | Cook time: 5 to 7 hours |
Serves 4 to 6

4 turkey drumsticks	3 tablespoons Worcestershire sauce
1 to 2 teaspoons salt	¾ teaspoon hickory smoke
¼ to ½ teaspoon pepper	2 tablespoons instant minced onion
85 g molasses	
60 ml vinegar	
120 g ketchup	

1. Sprinkle turkey with salt and pepper. Place in slow cooker.
2. Combine remaining ingredients. Pour over turkey.
3. Cover. Cook on low 5 to 7 hours.

Turkey in the Slow Cooker

Prep time: 5 minutes | Cook time: 1 to 5 hours |
Serves 6 to 8

1 (1.4 to 2.3 kg) bone-in turkey breast	2 carrots, cut in chunks
Salt and pepper to taste	1 onion, cut in eighths
	2 ribs celery, cut in chunks

1. Rinse turkey breast and pat dry. Season well inside with salt.
2. Place vegetables in bottom of slow cooker. Sprinkle with pepper. Place turkey breast on top of vegetables.
3. Cover and cook on high 1 to 3 hours, on low 4 to 5 hours, or until tender but not dry or mushy.

Cranberry-Orange Turkey Breast

Prep time: 10 minutes | Cook time: 3½ to 8 hours |
Serves 9

160 g orange marmalade	2 teaspoons orange zest, grated
1 (454 g) can whole cranberries in sauce	1 (1.4 kg) turkey breast

1. Combine marmalade, cranberries, and zest in a bowl.
2. Place the turkey breast in the slow cooker and pour half the orange-cranberry mixture over the turkey.
3. Cover. Cook on low 7 to 8 hours, or on high 3½ to 4 hours, until turkey juices run clear.
4. Add remaining half of orange-cranberry mixture for the last half hour of cooking.
5. Remove turkey to warm platter and allow to rest for 15 minutes before slicing.
6. Serve with orange-cranberry sauce.

Saucy Turkey Breast

Prep time: 5 minutes | Cook time: 1 to 5 hours |
Serves 6 to 8

1 (1.4 to 2.3 kg) bone-in or boneless turkey breast	1 (454 g) can cranberry sauce, jellied or whole-berry
1 envelope dry onion soup mix	2 tablespoons corn flour
Salt and pepper to taste	2 tablespoons cold water

1. Sprinkle salt and pepper and soup mix on the top and bottom of turkey breast. Place turkey in slow cooker.
2. Add cranberry sauce to top of turkey breast.
3. Cover and cook on low 4 to 5 hours, or on high 1 to 3 hours, or until tender but not dry and mushy. (A meat thermometer should read 82°C.)
4. Remove turkey from cooker and allow to rest for 10 minutes. (Keep sauce in cooker.)
5. Meanwhile, cover cooker and turn to high. In a small bowl, mix together corn flour and cold water until smooth. When sauce is boiling, stir in corn flour paste. Continue to simmer until sauce thickens.
6. Slice turkey and serve topped with sauce from cooker.

Beans with Kielbasa

Prep time: 10 minutes | Cook time: 6 to 8 hours |

Serves 8

1 medium green bell pepper, chopped
1 (439 g) can butter beans
1 (439 g) can pinto beans
1 (411 g) can low-sodium stewed tomatoes, or diced tomatoes with green chilies
1 (227 g) can low-sodium

tomato sauce
1 large onion, chopped
455 g reduced-fat smoked turkey kielbasa, cut in 1-inch pieces
1 clove garlic, minced
¼ teaspoon black pepper

1.Combine all ingredients in slow cooker.
2.Cover. Cook on low 6 to 8 hours.

Chicken Azteca

Prep time: 20 minutes | Cook time: 2½ to 6½ hours |

Serves 10 to 12

2 (425 g) cans black beans, drained
655 g frozen sweetcorn kernels
2 garlic cloves, minced
¾ teaspoon ground cumin
550 g chunky salsa, divided

10 skinless, boneless chicken breast halves
460 g cream cheese, cubed
Rice, cooked
Shredded Cheddar cheese

1.Combine beans, corn, garlic, cumin, and half of salsa in slow cooker.
2.Arrange chicken breasts over top. Pour remaining salsa over top.
3.Cover. Cook on high 2 to 3 hours, or on low 4 to 6 hours.
4.Remove chicken and cut into bite-sized pieces. Return to cooker.
5.Stir in cream cheese. Cook on high until cream cheese melts.
6.Spoon chicken and sauce over cooked rice. Top with shredded cheese.

Chickenetti

Prep time: 25 minutes | Cook time: 2 to 3 hours |

Serves 10

240 ml fat-free, low-sodium chicken broth
455 g spaghetti, cooked
560 – 840 g cubed and cooked chicken or turkey breast
1 (305 g) can fat-free, low-sodium cream of mushroom or celery soup

240 ml water
40 g chopped green bell peppers
50 g diced celery
½ teaspoon black pepper
1 medium onion, grated
230 g fat-free white or yellow American cheese, cubed

1.Put chicken broth into very large slow cooker. Add spaghetti and chicken.
2.In large bowl, combine soup and water until smooth. Stir in remaining ingredients; then pour into slow cooker.
3.Cover. Cook on low 2 to 3 hours.

Sauerkraut and Turkey Sausage

Prep time: 5 minutes | Cook time: 4 to 6 hours |

Serves 8

1 large can sauerkraut
55 -110 g brown sugar, according to your taste

preference
1 (8 inch) link spicy or smoked turkey sausage

1.Pour sauerkraut into slow cooker.
2.Sprinkle with brown sugar.
3.Cut turkey sausage into ¼-inch slices and arrange over sauerkraut.
4.Cook on low 4 to 6 hours.

Chicken and Prawn Jambalaya

Prep time: 15 minutes | Cook time: 2¼ to 3¾ hours |

Serves 5 to 6

1 (1.6 to 1.8 kg) roasting chicken, cut up
3 onions, diced
1 carrot, sliced
3 to 4 garlic cloves, minced
1 teaspoon dried oregano

1 teaspoon dried basil
1 teaspoon salt
⅛ teaspoon white pepper
1 (397 g) can crushed tomatoes
455 g shelled raw prawns
420 g rice, cooked

1.Combine all ingredients except prawns and rice in slow cooker.
2.Cover. Cook on low 2 to 3½ hours, or until chicken is tender.
3.Add prawns and rice.
4.Cover. Cook on high 15 to 20 minutes, or until prawns are done.

White Chicken Chili

Prep time: 25 minutes | Cook time: 3½ to 5 hours |

Serves 6 to 8

2 whole skinless chicken breasts
1.4 litres water
2 chopped onions
2 garlic cloves, minced
1 tablespoon oil
2 to 4 (113 g) cans chopped green chilies
1 to 2 diced jalapeño peppers

2 teaspoons ground cumin
1½ teaspoons dried oregano
¼ teaspoon cayenne pepper
½ teaspoon salt
1 (1.4 kg) can navy beans, undrained
120 to 240 g shredded cheese
Sour cream
Salsa

1.Place chicken in slow cooker. Add 1.4 litres water.
2.Cover. Cook on low 3 to 4 hours, or until tender.
3.Remove chicken from slow cooker. Cube and set aside.
4.Sauté onions and garlic in oil in a frying pan. Add chilies, jalapeño peppers, cumin, oregano, pepper, and salt. Sauté 2 minutes. Transfer to broth in slow cooker.
5.Add navy beans.
6.Cover. Cook on low 30 to 60 minutes.
7.Right before serving add chicken and cheese.
8.Serve topped with sour cream and salsa.

Sausage Pasta

Prep time: 20 minutes | Cook time: 8 to 10 hours | Serves 6

455 g turkey sausage, cut in 1-inch chunks
150 g chopped green and/or red bell peppers
100 g chopped celery
160 g chopped red onions
125 g chopped green courgette

1 (227 g) can tomato paste
480 ml water
1 (397 g) tomatoes, chopped
60 ml cooking wine
1 tablespoon Italian seasoning
455 g pasta, cooked

1. Combine all ingredients except pasta in slow cooker.
2. Cover. Cook on low 8 to 10 hours.
3. Add pasta 10 minutes before serving.

Chicken and Ham Gumbo

Prep time: 20 minutes | Cook time: 6 to 8 hours | Serves 4

680 g boneless, skinless chicken thighs, cubed
1 tablespoon oil
285 g frozen okra
230 g smoked ham, cut into small chunks
240 g coarsely chopped onions
225 g coarsely chopped green

peppers
2 or 3 (283 g) cans cannellini beans, drained
1.4 litres chicken broth
2 (283 g) cans diced tomatoes with green chilies
2 tablespoons chopped fresh coriander

1. Cook chicken pieces in oil in a frying pan until no longer pink.
2. Run hot water over okra until pieces separate easily.
3. Combine all ingredients but coriander in slow cooker.
4. Cover. Cook on low 6 to 8 hours. Stir in coriander before serving.

Mulligan Stew

Prep time: 15 minutes | Cook time: 7 hours | Serves 8 to 10

1 (1.4 kg) stewing hen, cut up, or 1.8 kg chicken legs and thighs
1½ teaspoons salt
115 g salt pork or bacon, cut in 1-inch squares
720 g tomatoes, peeled and sliced
330 g fresh sweetcorn, or 455 g

frozen sweetcorn
150 g coarsely chopped potatoes
285 g frozen lima beans
80 g chopped onions
1 teaspoon salt
¼ teaspoon pepper
Dash of cayenne pepper

1. Place chicken in very large slow cooker. Add water to cover. Add 1½ teaspoons salt.
2. Cover. Cook on low 2 hours. Add more water if needed.
3. Add remaining ingredients. (If you don't have a large cooker, divide the stew between 2 average-sized ones.) Simmer on low 5 hours longer.

Chicken and Vegetables

Prep time: 15 minutes | Cook time: 6 hours | Serves 4

1 (82 g) packages dry bearnaise sauce mix
120 ml dry white wine
455 g boneless, skinless chicken breasts, cut into bite-sized cubes
255 g frozen mixed vegetables
455 g cooked ham, cubed

455 g russet potatoes, cubed
1 red bell pepper, chopped
1 green bell pepper, chopped
3 shallots, minced
½ teaspoon garlic powder
½ teaspoon turmeric powder
½ teaspoon dried tarragon

1. Combine all ingredients in slow cooker.
2. Cover. Cook on low 6 hours.

Chicken Breasts with Rosemary

Prep time: 10 minutes | Cook time: 3 to 6 hours | Serves 4

4 boneless, skinless chicken breast halves (113 g each)
1½ teaspoons balsamic vinegar
1 teaspoon minced garlic
1 tablespoon grated lemon rind
¼ teaspoon salt

⅛ teaspoon black pepper
120 ml dry white wine or reduced-sodium chicken broth
1 teaspoon finely chopped fresh rosemary, or ½ teaspoon dried
90 g fresh diced tomato

1. Place chicken breasts in slow cooker.
2. Mix vinegar, garlic, lemon rind, salt, pepper, and wine. Pour over chicken.
3. Cover. Cook on low 6 hours, or on high 3 hours.
4. One-half hour before the end of the cooking time, stir in rosemary and fresh tomato.

Savory Stuffed Green Peppers

Prep time: 20 minutes | Cook time: 3 to 9 hours | Serves 8

8 small green peppers, tops removed and seeded
284 g frozen corn
340 g 99% fat-free minced turkey
340 g extra-lean minced beef
1 (227 g) can low-sodium tomato sauce
½ teaspoon garlic powder

¼ teaspoon black pepper
120 g shredded low-fat American cheese
½ teaspoon Worcestershire sauce
40 g chopped onions
3 tablespoons water
2 tablespoons ketchup

1. Wash peppers and drain well. Combine all ingredients except water and ketchup in mixing bowl. Stir well.
2. Stuff peppers ⅔ full.
3. Pour water in slow cooker. Arrange peppers on top.
4. Pour ketchup over peppers.
5. Cover. Cook on high 3 to 4 hours, or on low 7 to 9 hours.

Tender Turkey Breast

Prep time: 5 minutes | Cook time: 2 to 9 hours | Serves 10

1 (2.7 kg) boneless or bone-in turkey breast	2 to 3 tablespoons water

1. Place the turkey breast in the slow cooker. Add water.
2. Cover and cook on high 2 to 4 hours, or on low 4 to 9 hours, or until tender but not dry and mushy.
3. Turn over once during cooking time.
4. If you'd like to brown the turkey, place it in your oven and bake it uncovered at 165°C for 15 to 20 minutes after it's finished cooking in the slow cooker.

Can-You-Believe-It's-So-Simple Salsa Chicken

Prep time: 5 minutes | Cook time: 5 to 8 hours | Serves 4 to 6

4 to 6 boneless, skinless chicken breast halves
1 (454 g) jar chunky-style salsa, your choice of heat
240 g shredded cheese, your choice of flavor

1. Place chicken in slow cooker. Pour salsa over chicken.
2. Cover and cook on low 5 to 8 hours, or until chicken is tender but not dry.
3. Top individual servings with shredded cheese and serve.

Maple-Glazed Turkey Breast with Rice

Prep time: 15 minutes | Cook time: 4 to 6 hours | Serves 4

170 g long-grain wild rice mix	85 g maple syrup
360 ml water	1 onion, chopped
900 g boneless turkey breast, cut into 1½ to 2-inch chunks	¼ teaspoon ground cinnamon
	½ teaspoon salt (optional)

1. Combine all ingredients in the slow cooker.
2. Cook on low 4 to 6 hours, or until turkey and rice are both tender, but not dry and mushy.

Slow Cooker Stuffing with Poultry

Prep time: 15 minutes | Cook time: 7 to 9 hours | Serves 18

1 large loaf dried low-fat bread, cubed	55 g butter, melted
280 g chopped, cooked turkey or chicken, skin removed	960 ml fat-free chicken broth
1 large onion, chopped	1 tablespoon poultry seasoning
3 ribs celery with leaves, chopped	1 teaspoon salt
	4 eggs, beaten
	½ teaspoon black pepper

1. Mix together all ingredients. Pour into slow cooker.
2. Cover and cook on high 1 hour, then reduce to low 6 to 8 hours.

Low-Fat Chicken Cacciatore

Prep time: 15 minutes | Cook time: 8 hours | Serves 10

900 g uncooked boneless, skinless chicken breasts, cubed	tomato paste
225 g fresh mushrooms	1 (340 g) can low-sodium tomato sauce
1 bell pepper, chopped	½ teaspoon dried oregano
1 medium-sized onion, chopped	½ teaspoon dried basil
1 (340 g) can low-sodium chopped tomatoes	½ teaspoon garlic powder
1 (170 g) can low-sodium	½ teaspoon salt
	½ teaspoon black pepper

1. Combine all ingredients in slow cooker.
2. Cover. Cook on low 8 hours.
3. Serve.

Chapter 6 Pork

Black Beans with Ham

Prep time: 20 minutes | Cook time: 10 to 12 hours |
Serves 8 to 10

720 g dry black beans
145 to 290 g diced ham
1 teaspoon salt (optional)
1 teaspoon cumin
80 to 160 g minced onion

2 garlic cloves, minced
3 bay leaves
720 g diced tomatoes
1 tablespoon brown sugar

1. Cover black beans with water and soak for 8 hours, or overnight. Drain and pour beans into slow cooker.
2. Add all remaining ingredients and stir well. Cover with water.
3. Cover cooker. Cook on low 10 to 12 hours.
4. Serve.

Smothered Lentils

Prep time: 10 minutes | Cook time: 8 hours | Serves 6

520 g dry lentils, rinsed and sorted
1 medium onion, chopped
50 g chopped celery
2 garlic cloves, minced
146 g ham, cooked and chopped
75 g chopped carrots

180 g diced tomatoes
1 teaspoon dried marjoram
1 teaspoon ground coriander
Salt to taste
Pepper to taste
720 ml water

1. Combine all ingredients in slow cooker.
2. Cover. Cook on low 8 hours. (Check lentils after 5 hours of cooking. If they've absorbed all the water, stir in 240 ml more water.)

Sausage and Scalloped Potatoes

Prep time: 20 minutes | Cook time: 4 to 10 hours |
Serves 8

900 g potatoes, sliced ¼-inch thick, divided
455 g fully cooked smoked sausage link, sliced ½-inch thick, divided
2 medium-sized onions, chopped, divided

1 (305 g) can condensed Cheddar cheese soup, divided
1 (305 g) can condensed cream of celery soup
285 g frozen peas, thawed (optional)
Nonstick cooking spray

1. Spray interior of cooker with nonstick cooking spray.
2. Layer into the cooker one-third of the potatoes, one-third of the sausage, one-third of the onion, and one-third of the Cheddar cheese soup.

3. Repeat layers two more times.
4. Top with cream of celery soup.
5. Cover and cook on low 8 to 10 hours, or on high 4 to 5 hours, or until vegetables are tender.
6. If you wish, stir in peas. Cover and let stand 5 minutes. (If you forgot to thaw the peas, stir them in but let stand 10 minutes.)

Cranberry Ham

Prep time: 10 minutes | Cook time: 4½ hours |
Serves 4

1 (455 to 900 g) fully cooked ham, or 2-inch-thick slice of fully cooked ham

295 g whole cranberry sauce
2 tablespoons brown sugar

1. Place ham in slow cooker. Cover with cranberry sauce. Sprinkle brown sugar over top.
2. Cook on low 4½ hours, or until meat is heated through but not drying out.

Green Beans with Sausage

Prep time: 5 minutes | Cook time: 4 to 5 hours |
Serves 4 to 5

1 (454 g) package miniature smoked sausage links
600 g green beans, with most of the juice drained

1 small onion, chopped
105 g brown sugar
60 g ketchup

1. Place sausage in slow cooker. Top with beans and then onion.
2. In a bowl, stir together sugar and ketchup. Spoon over top.
3. Cover and cook on low 4 to 5 hours.

Creamy Scalloped Potatoes and Ham

Prep time: 20 minutes | Cook time: 4 to 5 hours |
Serves 6

1.5 kg sliced, raw potatoes
Salt and pepper to taste
1 (305 g) can cream of

mushroom or celery soup
360 ml milk
455 g cooked ham, cubed

1. Place potatoes in slow cooker. Sprinkle with salt and pepper each layer.
2. In a bowl, mix soup, milk, and ham together. Pour over potatoes.
3. Cover and cook on high for 3½ hours. Continue cooking ½ to 1½ hours more if needed, or until potatoes are tender.

Golden Autumn Stew

Prep time: 40 minutes | Cook time: 2 to 4 hours | Serves 8 to 10

300 g cubed Yukon gold potatoes
260 g cubed, peeled sweet potatoes
410 g cubed, peeled butternut squash
150 g cubed, peeled turnip
150 g diced carrots
100 g sliced celery
455 g smoked sausage
480 ml apple juice or cider
1 tart apple, thinly sliced
Salt to taste
Pepper to taste
1 tablespoon sugar or honey

1. Combine vegetables in slow cooker.
2. Place ring of sausage on top.
3. Add apple juice and apple slices.
4. Cover. Cook on high 2 hours and on low 4 hours, or until vegetables are tender. Do not stir.
5. To serve, remove sausage ring. Season with salt, pepper, and sugar as desired. Place vegetables in bowl. Slice meat into rings and place on top.
6. Serve.

Apple-Raisin Ham

Prep time: 15 minutes | Cook time: 4 to 5 hours | Serves 6

680 g fully cooked ham
1 (595 g) can apple pie filling
55 g golden raisins
80 ml orange juice
¼ teaspoon ground cinnamon
2 tablespoons water

1. Cut ham slices into six equal pieces.
2. In a mixing bowl, combine pie filling, raisins, orange juice, cinnamon, and water.
3. Place 1 slice of ham in your slow cooker. Spread ⅙ of the apple mixture over top.
4. Repeat layers until you have used all the ham and apple mixture.
5. Cover and cook on low 4 to 5 hours.

Scalloped Potatoes and Ham

Prep time: 20 minutes | Cook time: 6 to 8 hours | Serves 4 to 6

900 g to 1.4 kg potatoes, peeled, sliced, divided
340 to 455 g cooked ham, cubed, divided
1 small onion, chopped, divided
240 g shredded Cheddar cheese, divided
1 (305 g) can cream of celery or mushroom soup
Nonstick cooking spray

1. Spray the interior of the cooker with nonstick cooking spray.
2. Layer ⅓ each of the potatoes, ham, onion, and cheese into the cooker.
3. Repeat twice.
4. Spread soup on top.
5. Cover and cook on low 6 to 8 hours, or until potatoes are tender.

Sweet and Spicy Kielbasa

Prep time: 5 minutes | Cook time: 2½ to 3 hours | Serves 6 to 8

210 g brown sugar
1 tablespoon spicy mustard
900 g smoked fully cooked kielbasa, cut into 1-inch pieces

1. Combine brown sugar and mustard in slow cooker.
2. Add kielbasa; stir to coat evenly.
3. Cover and cook on low 2½ to 3 hours, stirring occasionally.

Sausage and Apples

Prep time: 10 minutes | Cook time: 1 to 3 hours | Serves 4

455 g smoked sausage
2 large apples, cored and sliced
55 g brown sugar
120 ml apple juice

1. Cut meat into 2-inch pieces.
2. Place all ingredients in slow cooker and mix together well.
3. Cover and cook on low 1 to 3 hours, or until heated through and until apples are as tender as you like them.

Sweet and Sour Sausage Dish

Prep time: 15 minutes | Cook time: 3 to 6 hours | Serves 8 to 10

2 (567 g) cans pineapple chunks, drained
2 large green peppers, sliced into bite-sized strips
455 g smoked sausage, cut into 1-inch chunks
1 (510 g) bottle honey barbecue sauce

1. Combine pineapples, peppers, and sausage chunks in slow cooker.
2. Pour barbecue sauce over mixture and stir.
3. Cover and cook on high 3 hours, or on low 6 hours, or until dish is heated through.

Sausage and Sweet Potatoes

Prep time: 20 minutes | Cook time: 4 to 10 hours | Serves 4 to 6

455 g bulk sausage
2 sweet potatoes, peeled and sliced
3 apples, peeled and sliced
2 tablespoons brown sugar
1 tablespoon plain flour
60 ml water

1. Brown loose sausage in a frying pan, breaking up chunks of meat with a wooden spoon. Drain.
2. Layer sausage, sweet potatoes, and apples in slow cooker.
3. Combine remaining ingredients and pour over ingredients in slow cooker.
4. Cover. Cook on low 8 to 10 hours, or on high 4 hours.

Ham and Chunky Potatoes

Prep time: 5 minutes | Cook time: 10 hours | Serves 6 to 8

6 to 8 medium red or russet potatoes, cut into chunks	ham
1 (900 g to 1.4 kg) boneless	105 g brown sugar
	1 teaspoon dry mustard

1. Prick potato pieces with fork. Place in slow cooker.
2. Place ham on top of potatoes. Crumble brown sugar over ham. Sprinkle with dry mustard.
3. Cover. Cook on low 10 or more hours, until potatoes are tender.
4. Pour juices over ham and potatoes to serve.

Potatoes and Green Beans with Ham

Prep time: 5 minutes | Cook time: 6 to 8 hours | Serves 4

455 g ham slice, cut in chunks	quartered, but not peeled
300 g green beans, frozen or fresh	120 ml water
300 g red-skinned potatoes,	80 g chopped onion
	4 slices American cheese

1. Place all ingredients, except cheese, in slow cooker. Gently mix together.
2. Cover and cook on low 6 to 8 hours, or until vegetables are tender.
3. One hour before the end of the cooking time, lay cheese slices over top.

Ham-Yam-Apple

Prep time: 10 minutes | Cook time: 4 to 5 hours | Serves 4

1 slice fully cooked ham (about 455 g)	2 apples, thinly sliced
1 (822 g) can sweet potatoes or yams, drained	55 g light brown sugar
	2 tablespoons orange juice

1. Cube ham.
2. Combine all ingredients in slow cooker.
3. Cook on low 4 to 5 hours, or until apples are tender.

Ham and Cabbage

Prep time: 30 minutes | Cook time: 6 to 7 hours | Serves 4

900 g uncooked ham	1 medium head green cabbage
12 whole cloves	Water
8 medium red potatoes	

1. Rinse ham, then stick cloves evenly into ham. Place in center of slow cooker.
2. Cut potatoes in half. Add to slow cooker around the ham.
3. Quarter cabbage and remove center stem. Add to cooker, again surrounding the ham.
4. Fill with water to cover.
5. Cover and cook on high 6 to 7 hours, or until vegetables and meat are tender, but not dry or mushy.
6. Serve.

Ham-Broccoli Casserole

Prep time: 20 minutes | Cook time: 4 to 5 hours | Serves 4

455 g frozen broccoli cuts, thawed and drained	115 g of your favorite mild cheese, cubed
290 to 435 g cubed, cooked ham	240 ml milk
1 (305 g) can cream of mushroom soup	210 g instant rice, uncooked
	1 rib celery, chopped
	1 small onion, chopped

1. Combine broccoli and ham in slow cooker.
2. Combine soup, cheese, milk, rice, celery, and onion. Stir into broccoli.
3. Cover. Cook on low 4 to 5 hours.

Ham and Lima Beans

Prep time: 15 minutes | Cook time: 4 to 7 hours | Serves 6

455 g dry lima beans	1 teaspoon pepper
1 onion, chopped	230 g ham, finely cubed
1 bell pepper, chopped	240 ml water
1 teaspoon dry mustard	1 (305 g) can tomato soup
1 teaspoon salt	

1. Cover beans with water. Soak 8 hours. Drain.
2. Combine all ingredients in slow cooker.
3. Cover. Cook on low 7 hours, or on high 4 hours.
4. If mixture begins to dry out, add 120 ml water or more and stir well.
5. Serve.

Ham with Sweet Potatoes and Oranges

Prep time: 15 minutes | Cook time: 7 to 8 hours | Serves 4

2 to 3 sweet potatoes, peeled and sliced ¼-inch thick	3 tablespoons orange juice concentrate
1 large ham slice	3 tablespoons honey
3 seedless oranges, peeled and sliced	105 g brown sugar
	2 tablespoons corn flour

1. Place sweet potatoes in slow cooker.
2. Arrange ham and orange slices on top.
3. Combine remaining ingredients. Drizzle over ham and oranges.
4. Cover. Cook on low 7 to 8 hours.
5. Serve.

Verenike Casserole

Prep time: 15 minutes | Cook time: 5 to 6 hours |
Serves 8 to 10

680 g cottage cheese	225 g sour cream
3 eggs	480 ml evaporated milk
1 teaspoon salt	290 g cubed cooked ham
½ teaspoon pepper	7 to 9 dry lasagna noodles

1.Combine all ingredients except noodles.
2.Place half of creamy ham mixture in bottom of cooker. Add uncooked noodles. Cover with remaining half of creamy ham sauce. Be sure noodles are fully submerged in sauce.
3.Cover. Cook on low 5 to 6 hours.
4.Serve.

Shepherd's Pie

Prep time: 40 minutes | Cook time: 3 hours | Serves
3 to 4

455 g minced pork	1 small onion, chopped
1 tablespoon vinegar	1 (425 g) can corn, drained
1¼ teaspoons salt, divided	3 large potatoes
¼ teaspoon hot pepper	60 ml milk
1 teaspoon paprika	1 teaspoon butter
¼ teaspoon dried oregano	Dash of pepper
¼ teaspoon black pepper	Shredded cheese
1 teaspoon chili powder	

1.Combine pork, vinegar, and spices except ¼ teaspoon salt. Cook in a frying pan until brown. Add onion and cook until onions begin to glaze. Spread in bottom of slow cooker.
2.Spread corn over meat.
3.Boil potatoes until soft. Mash with milk, butter, ¼ teaspoon salt, and dash of pepper. Spread over meat and corn.
4.Cover. Cook on low 3 hours. Sprinkle top with cheese a few minutes before serving.

Ham Loaf or Balls

Prep time: 30 minutes | Cook time: 4 to 6 hours |
Serves 8 to 10

Ham Loaf or Balls:	1¼ teaspoons salt
455 g chopped ham	⅛ teaspoon pepper
455 g minced pork or minced beef	Glaze:
60 g soft bread crumbs	160 g brown sugar
2 eggs, slightly beaten	1 teaspoon dry mustard
240 ml milk	1 tablespoon corn flour
2 tablespoons minced onions	60 ml vinegar
	120 ml water

1.Combine ham loaf or balls ingredients. Form into loaf or balls and place in slow cooker.
2.Combine dry ingredients for glaze in bowl. Mix in vinegar and water until smooth. Pour into saucepan. Cook until slightly thickened. Pour over meat.
3.Cover. Cook on high 4 to 6 hours.

Kielbasa Stew

Prep time: 45 minutes | Cook time: 8 to 10 hours |
Serves 6 to 8

6 strips of bacon	chilies
1 onion, chopped	2 medium carrots, thinly sliced
680 g smoked, fully cooked kielbasa, thinly sliced	1 medium green pepper, chopped
2 (439 g) cans butter beans	½ teaspoon Italian seasoning
2 (227 g) cans tomato sauce	½ teaspoon dried thyme
1 (113 g) can chopped green	½ teaspoon black pepper

1.Fry bacon in a frying pan until crisp. Crumble bacon and place in large slow cooker. Add onions and kielbasa to drippings in frying pan. Cook until onions are soft.
2.Transfer onions and kielbasa to slow cooker.
3.Add all remaining ingredients to cooker and stir together well.
4.Cover. Cook on low 8 to 10 hours, or until vegetables are tender.

Rice and Beans—and Sausage

Prep time: 25 minutes | Cook time: 4 to 6 hours |
Serves 8

3 celery ribs, chopped	¼ teaspoon red pepper flakes
1 onion, chopped	¼ teaspoon pepper
2 garlic cloves, minced	230 g fully cooked smoked
420 ml tomato juice	turkey sausage or kielbasa, cut
2 (454 g) cans kidney beans, drained	into ¼-inch slices
¾ teaspoon dried oregano	840 g rice, cooked
¾ teaspoon dried thyme	Shredded cheese (optional)

1.Combine all ingredients except rice and shredded cheese in slow cooker.
2.Cover. Cook on low 4 to 6 hours.
3.Serve over rice. Garnish with shredded cheese, if you wish.

Economy One-Dish Supper

Prep time: 15 minutes | Cook time: 4 to 10 hours |
Serves 6

230 g lean sausage	1 onion, minced
225 g potatoes, grated or cubed	¼ teaspoon salt
240 ml water	¼ teaspoon black pepper
½ teaspoon cream of tartar	¼ teaspoon curry powder
170 g raw carrots, grated or thinly sliced	720 ml low-sodium tomato juice
55 g rice, uncooked	

1.Brown sausage in nonstick frying pan. Cut into ¼-inch-thick slices.
2.Mix water and cream of tartar. Toss with potatoes. Drain.
3.Layer sausage, potatoes, carrots, rice, and onion in slow cooker.
4.Combine salt, pepper, curry powder, and tomato juice. Pour over all.
5.Cover. Cook on low 8 to 10 hours, or on high 4 to 5 hours.

Bandito Chili Dogs

Prep time: 10 minutes | Cook time: 3 to 3½ hours |
Serves 10

455 g hot dogs	chilies
2 (425 g) cans chili, with or without beans	10 hot dog buns
	1 medium onion, chopped
1 (305 g) can condensed Cheddar cheese soup	35 to 70 g corn chips, coarsely crushed
1 (113 g) can chopped green	120 g shredded Cheddar cheese

1. Place hot dogs in slow cooker.
2. Combine chili, soup, and green chilies. Pour over hot dogs.
3. Cover. Cook on low 3 to 3½ hours.
4. Serve hot dogs in buns. Top with chili mixture, onion, corn chips, and cheese.

Chili Hot Dogs

Prep time: 10 minutes | Cook time: 2 to 3 hours |
Serves 4 to 5

1 package hot dogs, cut into ¾-inch slices	1 teaspoon prepared mustard
	1 teaspoon instant minced onion
1 (794 g) can baked beans	95 g chili sauce

1. In slow cooker, combine all ingredients.
2. Cover and cook on low 2 to 3 hours.
3. Serve.

Harvest Kielbasa

Prep time: 20 minutes | Cook time: 4 to 8 hours |
Serves 6

900 g smoked kielbasa	105 g brown sugar
750 g unsweetened applesauce	3 medium onions, sliced

1. Slice kielbasa into ¼-inch slices. Brown in a frying pan. Drain.
2. Combine applesauce and brown sugar.
3. Layer kielbasa, onions, and applesauce mixture in slow cooker.
4. Cover. Cook on low 4 to 8 hours.

Apricot-Glazed Ham

Prep time: 20 minutes | Cook time: 4 to 6 hours |
Serves 4

4 ham steaks	like
95 g apricot jam	80 ml soy sauce
255 to 340 g honey, depending upon how much sweetness you	¼ teaspoon nutmeg

1. Place ham in slow cooker.
2. In a bowl, mix all other ingredients together. Pour over ham.
3. Cook on low 4 to 6 hours, or until meat is heated through but not dry.

Polish Sausage Stew

Prep time: 15 minutes | Cook time: 4 to 8 hours |
Serves 6 to 8

1 (305 g) can cream of celery soup
70 g packed brown sugar
1 (765 g) can sauerkraut, drained
680 g Polish sausage, cut into 2-inch pieces and browned
4 medium potatoes, cubed
160 g chopped onions
120 g shredded Monterey Jack cheese

1. Combine soup, sugar, and sauerkraut. Stir in sausage, potatoes, and onions.
2. Cover. Cook on low 8 hours, or on high 4 hours.
3. Stir in cheese and serve.

Sausage-Sauerkraut Supper

Prep time: 20 minutes | Cook time: 8 to 9 hours |
Serves 10 to 12

600 g cubed carrots	1 medium onion, thinly sliced
600 g cubed red potatoes	3 garlic cloves, minced
2 (397 g) cans sauerkraut, rinsed and drained	360 ml dry white wine or chicken broth
1.1 kg fresh Polish sausage, cut into 3-inch pieces	½ teaspoon pepper
	1 teaspoon caraway seeds

1. Layer carrots, potatoes, and sauerkraut in slow cooker.
2. Brown sausage in a frying pan. Transfer to slow cooker. Reserve 1 tablespoon drippings in frying pan.
3. Sauté onion and garlic in drippings until tender. Stir in wine. Bring to boil. Stir to loosen brown bits. Stir in pepper and caraway seeds. Pour over sausage.
4. Cover. Cook on low 8 to 9 hours.

Ham and Cheese Casserole

Prep time: 30 minutes | Cook time: 2 to 4 hours |
Serves 8 to 10

1 (454 g) package medium egg noodles, divided	290 g fully cooked ham, cubed, divided
1 (305 g) can condensed cream of celery soup	240 g shredded cheese, your choice, divided
450 g sour cream	

1. Prepare noodles according to package instructions. Drain.
2. In a small bowl combine soup and sour cream until smooth. Set aside.
3. In a greased slow cooker, layer one-third of the cooked noodles, one-third of the ham, and one-third of the cheese.
4. Top with one-fourth of soup mixture.
5. Repeat steps 3 and 4 twice until all ingredients are used. The final layer should be the soup-sour cream mixture.
6. Cook 2 to 4 hours on low, or until heated through.

Saucy Hot Dogs

Prep time: 15 minutes | Cook time: 2 hours | Serves 8

455 g all-beef hot dogs
1 (283 g) jar grape jelly
80 g prepared mustard

60 ml red wine
¼ teaspoon dry mustard

1. Cut hot dogs into ½-inch slices. Place in slow cooker.
2. Mix remaining ingredients together with the hot dogs in the cooker.
3. Cover and cook on low for 2 hours.
4. Serve.

Ham Barbecue

Prep time: 5 minutes | Cook time: 8 hours | Serves 6 to 8

455 g boiled ham, cut into cubes

240 ml cola-flavored soda
235 g ketchup

1. Place ham in slow cooker. Pour soda and ketchup over ham.
2. Cover. Cook on low 8 hours.
3. Serve.

Creamy Sausage and Potatoes

Prep time: 15 minutes | Cook time: 6 to 8 hours | Serves 6

1.4 kg small potatoes, peeled and quartered
455 g smoked sausage, cut into ¼-inch slices
1 (227 g) package cream

cheese, softened
1 (305 g) can cream of celery soup
1 envelope dry ranch salad dressing mix

1. Place potatoes in slow cooker. Add sausage.
2. In a bowl, beat together cream cheese, soup, and salad dressing mix until smooth. Pour over potatoes and sausage.
3. Cover and cook on low 6 to 8 hours, or until the potatoes are tender, stirring half-way through cooking time if you're home. Stir again before serving.

Sausage and a Rainbow of Peppers

Prep time: 30 minutes | Cook time: 6 hours | Serves 8 to 10

3 medium onions, sliced
1 sweet red pepper, sliced
1 sweet green pepper, sliced
1 sweet yellow pepper, sliced
4 garlic cloves, minced
1 tablespoon oil

1 (794 g) can chopped tomatoes
1 teaspoon salt
½ teaspoon red crushed pepper
900 g to 1.4 kg sweet Italian sausage, cut into (3-inch) pieces

1. Sauté onions, peppers, and garlic in oil in a frying pan. When just softened, place in slow cooker.
2. Add tomatoes, salt, and crushed red pepper. Mix well.
3. Add sausage links.
4. Cover. Cook on low 6 hours.

5. Serve.

Chili Casserole

Prep time: 25 minutes | Cook time: 7 hours | Serves 6

455 g bulk pork sausage, browned
480 ml water
1 (439 g) can chili beans
1 (411 g) can diced tomatoes
155 g brown rice
40 g chopped onions

1 tablespoon chili powder
1 teaspoon Worcestershire sauce
1 teaspoon prepared mustard
¾ teaspoon salt
⅛ teaspoon garlic powder
120 g shredded Cheddar cheese

1. Combine all ingredients except cheese in slow cooker.
2. Cover. Cook on low 7 hours.
3. Stir in cheese during last 10 minutes of cooking time.

Sausage-Pasta Stew

Prep time: 35 minutes | Cook time: 7¼ to 9¼ hours | Serves 8

455 g Italian sausage, casings removed
960 ml water
1 (737 g) jar meatless spaghetti sauce
1 (454 g) can kidney beans, rinsed and drained
1 medium yellow summer squash, cut in 1-inch pieces
2 medium carrots, cut in ¼-inch

slices
1 medium red or green sweet pepper, diced
55 g chopped onions
190 g spiral pasta, uncooked
140 g frozen peas
1 teaspoon sugar
½ teaspoon salt
¼ teaspoon pepper

1. Sauté sausage in a frying pan until no longer pink. Drain and place in slow cooker.
2. Add water, spaghetti sauce, kidney beans, squash, carrots, pepper, and onions. Mix well.
3. Cover. Cook on low 7 to 9 hours, or until vegetables are tender.
4. Add remaining ingredients. Mix well.
5. Cover. Cook on high 15 to 20 minutes until pasta is tender.

Melt-in-Your-Mouth Sausages

Prep time: 5 minutes | Cook time: 6 to 8 hours | Serves 6 to 8

900 g sweet Italian sausage, cut into 5-inch lengths
1 (1.4 kg) jar spaghetti sauce
1 (170 g) can tomato paste
1 large green pepper, thinly sliced
1 large onion, thinly sliced

1 tablespoon grated Parmesan cheese
1 teaspoon dried parsley, or
1 tablespoon chopped fresh parsley
240 ml water

1. Place sausage in a frying pan. Cover with water. Simmer 10 minutes. Drain.
2. Combine remaining ingredients in slow cooker. Add sausage.
3. Cover. Cook on low 6 hours.
4. Serve.

Spiced Hot Dogs

Prep time: 5 minutes | Cook time: 2 hours | Serves 3 to 4

455 g hot dogs, cut in pieces
2 tablespoons brown sugar
3 tablespoons vinegar
115 g ketchup

2 teaspoons prepared mustard
120 ml water
80 g chopped onions

1.Place hot dogs in slow cooker.
2.Combine all ingredients except hot dogs in saucepan. Simmer. Pour over hot dogs.
3.Cover. Cook on low 2 hours.

Barbecued Hot Dogs

Prep time: 5 minutes | Cook time: 4½ hours | Serves 8

285 g apricot preserves
115 g tomato sauce
80 ml vinegar
2 tablespoons soy sauce
2 tablespoons honey

1 tablespoon oil
1 teaspoon salt
¼ teaspoon ground ginger
900 g hot dogs, cut into 1-inch pieces

1.Combine all ingredients except hot dogs in slow cooker.
2.Cover. Cook on high 30 minutes. Add hot dog pieces. Cook on low 4 hours.
3.Serve as an appetizer.

Bits and Bites

Prep time: 5 minutes | Cook time: 3 to 4 hours |
Serves 12

1 (330 ml) can beer
235 g ketchup
210 g light brown sugar
140 to 280 g barbecue sauce

455 g all-beef hot dogs, sliced
1½-inches thick
900 g cocktail sausages

1.Combine beer, ketchup, brown sugar, and barbecue sauce. Pour into slow cooker.
2.Add hot dogs and sausages. Mix well.
3.Cover. Cook on low 3 to 4 hours.

Bratwurst Stew

Prep time: 15 minutes | Cook time: 3 to 4 hours |
Serves 8

2 (305 g) cans fat-free chicken broth
4 medium carrots, sliced
2 ribs of celery, cut in chunks
1 medium onion, chopped
1 teaspoon dried basil

½ teaspoon garlic powder
270 g chopped cabbage
2 (454 g) cans butter beans, drained
5 fully cooked bratwurst links, cut into ½-inch slices

1.Combine all ingredients in slow cooker.
2.Cook on high 3 to 4 hours, or until veggies are tender.

Italian Sausage Dinner

Prep time: 10 minutes | Cook time: 5 to 10 hours |
Serves 6

680 g Italian sausage, cut in ¾-inch slices
2 tablespoons A-1 steak sauce
1 (794 g) can diced Italian-style tomatoes, with juice

2 chopped green peppers
½ teaspoon red pepper flakes (optional)
420 g minute rice, uncooked

1.Place all ingredients, except rice, in slow cooker.
2.Cover and cook on low 7½ to 9½ hours, or on high 4½ hours.
3.Stir in uncooked rice. Cover and cook an additional 20 minutes on high or low.

Bratwursts

Prep time: 15 minutes | Cook time: 4 to 5 hours |
Serves 8

8 bratwursts
1 large onion, sliced
1 (330 ml) can of beer
280 g chili sauce
1 tablespoon Worcestershire sauce

235 g ketchup
2 tablespoons vinegar
½ teaspoon salt
2 tablespoons brown sugar
1 tablespoon paprika

1.Boil bratwursts in water in a frying pan for 10 minutes to remove fat.
2.Drain bratwursts and place in slow cooker.
3.Mix together remaining ingredients in bowl and then pour over meat.
4.Cook on low 4 to 5 hours.

Election Lunch

Prep time: 30 minutes | Cook time: 2 to 4 hours |
Serves 6 to 12

2 to 3 tablespoons olive oil
1 large onion, chopped
455 g sausage, cut into thin slices, or casings removed and crumbled
1 rib celery, sliced
1 tablespoon Worcestershire sauce
1½ teaspoons dry mustard
85 g honey

1 (283 g) can tomatoes with green chili peppers
1 (454 g) can lima or butter beans, drained, with liquid reserved
1 (454 g) can red kidney beans, drained, with liquid reserved
1 (454 g) can garbanzo beans, drained, with liquid reserved

1.Brown onion and sausage in oil.
2.Combine ingredients in 6-quart slow cooker, or divide between 2 (4-quart) cookers and stir to combine. Add reserved juice from lima, kidney, and garbanzo beans if there's enough room in the cookers.
3.Cover. Cook on low 2 to 4 hours.

Kielbasa and Cabbage

Prep time: 15 minutes | Cook time: 7 to 8 hours |
Serves 6

1 (680 g) head green cabbage, shredded
2 medium onions, chopped
3 medium red potatoes, peeled and cubed
1 red bell pepper, chopped
2 garlic cloves, minced
160 ml dry white wine

680 g Polish kielbasa, cut into 3-inch long links
1 (794 g) can cut-up tomatoes with juice
1 tablespoon Dijon mustard
¾ teaspoon caraway seeds
½ teaspoon pepper
¾ teaspoon salt

1. Combine all ingredients in slow cooker.
2. Cover. Cook on low 7 to 8 hours, or until cabbage is tender.

Cranberry Franks

Prep time: 10 minutes | Cook time: 1 to 2 hours |
Serves 15 to 20

2 packages cocktail wieners or little smoked sausages
1 (454 g) can jellied cranberry sauce

235 g ketchup
3 tablespoons brown sugar
1 tablespoon lemon juice

1. Combine all ingredients in slow cooker.
2. Cover. Cook on high 1 to 2 hours.

Sausage in Spaghetti Sauce

Prep time: 15 minutes | Cook time: 3 to 6 hours |
Serves 10 to 12

1.8 kg sausage of your choice
1 red bell pepper
1 green bell pepper

1 large onion
1 (737 g) jar spaghetti sauce

1. Heat nonstick frying pan over medium-high heat. Brown sausage in nonstick frying pan in batches. As a batch is finished browning on all sides, cut into 1½-inch chunks. Then place in slow cooker.
2. Slice or chop peppers and onion and put on top of sausage.
3. Add spaghetti sauce over all.
4. Cover and cook on low 6 hours, or on high 3 hours.

Italian Spaghetti Sauce

Prep time: 20 minutes | Cook time: 8 to 9 hours |
Serves 8 to 10

900 g sausage or minced beef
3 medium onions, chopped
150 g sliced mushrooms
6 garlic cloves, minced
2 (411 g) cans diced tomatoes, undrained
1 (822 g) can tomato sauce

1 (340 g) can tomato paste
2 tablespoons dried basil
1 tablespoon dried oregano
1 tablespoon sugar
1 teaspoon salt
½ teaspoon crushed red pepper

flakes

1. Cook sausage, onions, mushrooms, and garlic in a frying pan over medium heat for 10 minutes. Drain. Transfer to slow cooker.
2. Stir in remaining ingredients.
3. Cover. Cook on low 8 to 9 hours.

Aunt Lavina's Sauerkraut

Prep time: 10 minutes | Cook time: 3 to 6 hours |
Serves 8 to 12

900 g to 1.4 kg smoked sausage, cut into 1-inch pieces
2 tablespoons water or oil
2 bell peppers, chopped
2 onions, sliced
230 g fresh mushrooms, sliced

570 g sauerkraut, drained
2 (411 g) cans diced tomatoes with green peppers
1 teaspoon salt
½ teaspoon pepper
2 tablespoons brown sugar

1. Place sausage in slow cooker. Heat on low while you prepare other ingredients.
2. Sauté peppers, onions, and mushrooms in small amount of water or oil in saucepan.
3. Combine all ingredients in slow cooker.
4. Cover. Cook on low 5 to 6 hours, or on high 3 to 4 hours.
5. Serve.

Sausage-Vegetable Stew

Prep time: 30 minutes | Cook time: 3 to 10 hours |
Serves 10

455 g sausage (regular, turkey, or smoked)
600 g potatoes, cooked and cubed
600 g carrots, cooked and sliced

600 g green beans, cooked
1 (794 g) can tomato sauce
1 teaspoon onion powder
¼ or ½ teaspoon black pepper, according to your taste

1. Slice sausage into 1½-inch pieces. Place in slow cooker.
2. Add cooked vegetables. Pour tomato sauce over top.
3. Sprinkle with onion powder and pepper. Stir.
4. Cook on high 3 to 4 hours, or on low 8 to 10 hours.

Frankwiches

Prep time: 15 minutes | Cook time: 4¼ hours |
Serves 16 to 18

2 (305 g) cans Cheddar cheese soup
80 g finely chopped onions
130 g sweet pickle relish

4 teaspoons prepared mustard
900 g hot dogs, thinly sliced
1 (225g) container sour cream

1. Combine soup, onions, relish, and mustard. Stir in sliced hot dogs.
2. Cover. Cook on low 4 hours.
3. Stir in sour cream.
4. Cover. Cook on high 10 to 15 minutes, stirring occasionally.
5. Serve.

Pot-Luck Wiener Bake

Prep time: 8 minutes | Cook time: 3 hours | Serves 6

600 g cooked potatoes, peeled
and diced
1 (305 g) can cream of
mushroom soup

230 g mayonnaise
145 g sauerkraut, drained
455 g wieners, sliced

1. Mix all ingredients in slow cooker.
2. Cover and cook on low 3 hours.

Hot Dogs and Noodles

Prep time: 25 minutes | Cook time: 5 to 6 hours | Serves 6

1 (227 g) package medium egg
noodles, cooked and drained
190 g grated Parmesan cheese
240 ml milk
55 g butter or margarine, melted
1 tablespoon plain flour

¼ teaspoon salt
1 (454 g) package hot dogs,
sliced
55 g packed brown sugar
55 g mayonnaise
2 tablespoons prepared mustard

1. Place noodles, cheese, milk, butter, flour, and salt in slow cooker. Mix well.
2. Combine hot dogs with remaining ingredients. Spoon evenly over noodles.
3. Cover. Cook on low 5 to 6 hours.

Frankfurter Succotash

Prep time: 10 minutes | Cook time: 4 to 6 hours | Serves 4 to 6

455 g hot dogs, cut into ½-inch slices
2 (283 g) packs frozen mixed beans, thawed and drained
1 (305 g) can Cheddar cheese soup

1. Stir all ingredients together in slow cooker.
2. Cover and cook on low 4 to 6 hours, or until vegetables are tender.

Barbecued Bacon and Beans

Prep time: 20 minutes | Cook time: 3 to 8 hours | Serves 4 to 6

455 g bacon
40 g chopped onions
175 g ketchup
105 g brown sugar

3 teaspoons Worcestershire
sauce
¾ teaspoon salt
600 g green beans

1. Brown bacon in a frying pan until crisp and then break into pieces. Reserve 2 tablespoons bacon drippings.
2. Sauté onions in bacon drippings.
3. Combine ketchup, brown sugar, Worcestershire sauce, and salt. Stir into bacon and onions.
4. Pour mixture over green beans and mix lightly.
5. Pour into slow cooker and cook on high 3 to 4 hours, or on low 6 to 8 hours.

Slow Cooker Stuffing with Sausage

Prep time: 40 minutes | Cook time: 4 hours | Serves 10

1.8 kg toasted bread crumbs or
dressing mix
455 g bulk sausage, browned
and drained
55 to 225 g butter (enough to
flavor bread)
160 g or more finely chopped
onions
100 g or more finely chopped
celery

1 (227 g) can sliced mushrooms,
with liquid
4 g chopped fresh parsley
2 teaspoons poultry seasoning
(omit if using dressing mix)
Dash of pepper
½ teaspoon salt
2 eggs, beaten
720 ml chicken stock

1. Combine bread crumbs and sausage.
2. Melt butter in a frying pan. Add onions and celery and sauté until tender. Stir in mushrooms and parsley. Add seasonings. Pour over bread crumbs and mix well.
3. Stir in eggs and chicken stock.
4. Pour into slow cooker and cook on high 1 hour, and on low an additional 3 hours.

Chapter 7 Staples, Sauces, Dips and Dressings

Taco Pizza Dip

Prep time: 15 minutes | Cook time: 1½ to 2 hours | Serves 8 to 10

2 (250 g) packages soft white cheese, softened	Half an envelope dry taco seasoning mix
225 to 340 g container French onion dip	225 g shredded Cheddar cheese
450 g minced beef	Green pepper, diced (optional)
	Mushrooms, sliced (optional)

1. Combine soft white cheese and onion dip. Spread in slow cooker.
2. Brown minced beef in a skillet or frying pan. Drain. Stir taco seasoning into meat.
3. Place seasoned meat on top of soft white cheese mixture.
4. Sprinkle Cheddar cheese on top of meat. Top with peppers and mushrooms, if you wish.
5. Cover and cook on low 1½ to 2 hours. Serve.

Creamy Taco Dip

Prep time: 15 minutes | Cook time: 2 to 3 hours | Serves 10 to 12

700 g minced beef	1 (450 g) jar of salsa
1 envelope dry taco seasoning mix	500 ml sour cream
	225 g shredded Cheddar cheese

1. Brown minced beef in non-stick skillet or frying pan. Drain.
2. Return beef to skillet or frying pan. Add taco seasoning and salsa.
3. Remove from stove and add sour cream and cheese. Pour mixture into slow cooker.
4. Cover and cook on low 2 to 3 hours, or until hot.
5. Serve.

Tomatoes and Chilli Cheese Dip

Prep time: 10 minutes | Cook time: 1 hour | Serves 10 to 12

450 g lean minced beef	2 teaspoons Worcestershire sauce
450 g Processed cheese, cubed	½ teaspoon chilli powder
1 (225 to 300 g) can tomatoes and green chillies	

1. Brown minced beef in non-stick skillet or frying pan. Drain.
2. Place browned beef in slow cooker. Add all remaining ingredients. Stir well.
3. Cover and cook on high 1 hour, stirring occasionally until cheese is fully melted.
4. Serve immediately or turn to low for serving up to 6 hours later.

Cheese, Crab, and Prawn Dip

Prep time: 10 minutes | Cook time: 2 hours | Serves 10 to 12

3 (250 g) packages soft white cheese, at room temperature	6 tablespoons finely chopped onions
3 ½ (100 g) cans crab meat, drained	1 teaspoon horseradish
150 g prawn, drained	115 g toasted almonds, broken

1. Combine all ingredients in slow cooker.
2. Cover. Cook on low 2 hours.
3. Serve.

Prairie Fire Dip

Prep time: 5 minutes | Cook time: 1 to 3 hours | Serves 10

235 g fat-free refried beans	1 tablespoon minced onion
115 g shredded fat-free Monterey Jack cheese	1 clove garlic, minced
60 ml water	2 teaspoons chilli powder
	Hot sauce as desired

1. Combine all ingredients in slow cooker.
2. Cover. Cook on high 1 hour, or on low 2 to 3 hours. Serve.

Curried Cheese Dip

Prep time: 10 minutes | Cook time: 1 hour | Serves 9 to 10

450 g shredded Cheddar cheese	125 ml milk
1 (250 g) package soft white cheese, softened	60 g chopped spring onions
	1½ teaspoons curry powder

1. Mix ingredients together in slow cooker.
2. Cover and heat on high 45 minutes to 1 hour, or until cheeses are melted and dip is heated through. Stir occasionally.
3. Turn cooker to low and serve.

Easy Refried Bean Dip

Prep time: 10 minutes | Cook time: 1½ hours |
Serves 12

2 (435 g) cans refried beans
1 envelope taco seasoning mix
(use all, or ¾, depending on
your taste preference)
115 g chopped onions
225 g shredded Monterey Jack

or Mexican Blend cheese
Chopped jalapeños or mild
chillies, to taste
2 to 4 drops Tabasco sauce
(optional)

1. Place beans, taco seasoning, onions, and cheese in your slow cooker. Stir well to blend.
2. Stir in jalapeños or chillies and Tabasco sauce.
3. Cook on low until cheese is melted, about 1½ hours.
4. Add a little water if the dip seems too thick.

Fiesta Dip

Prep time: 10 minutes | Cook time: 30 to 60 minutes
| Serves 8

1 (435 g) can refried beans
225 g shredded Cheddar cheese
115 g Mexican salsa

1 green chilli pepper, chopped
(optional)

1. Combine all ingredients and place in slow cooker.
2. Cover and heat 30 to 60 minutes, or until cheese is melted.
3. Serve.

Cheesy Bean Dip

Prep time: 10 minutes | Cook time: 1½ to 3 hours |
Serves 18 to 20

1 (435 g) can refried beans
2 (250 g) packages soft white
cheese, cubed
450 g salsa, your choice of heat

450 g shredded Cheddar cheese
1 envelope dry taco seasoning
mix

1. Mix all ingredients in slow cooker. Stir to combine well.
2. Cover and heat on high for 1½ hours, or on low for 3 hours, stirring occasionally. Serve.

Championship Bean Dip

Prep time: 10 minutes | Cook time: 2 hours | Makes 1 kg

1 (435 g) can refried beans
250 ml picante or hot pepper
sauce
225 g shredded Monterey Jack
cheese

225 g shredded Cheddar cheese
175 ml sour cream
85 g soft white cheese, softened
1 tablespoon chilli powder
¼ teaspoon ground cumin

1. In a bowl, combine all ingredients and transfer to slow cooker.
2. Cover. Cook on high 2 hours, or until heated through, stirring once or twice.
3. Serve.

Wide-Awake Refried Bean Dip

Prep time: 10 minutes | Cook time: 2 to 2½ hours |
Serves 8 to 10

565 g refried beans
225 g shredded Cheddar or hot
pepper cheese
115 g chopped spring onions

¼ teaspoon salt
2 to 4 tablespoons bottled taco
sauce (depending on your taste
preference)

1. In slow cooker, combine beans with cheese, onions, salt, and taco sauce.
2. Cover and cook on low 2 to 2½ hours.
3. Serve hot.

Irresistible Cheesy Hot Bean Dip

Prep time: 10 minutes | Cook time: 2 hours | Makes
1 to 1.2 kg

1 (435 g) can refried beans
225 g salsa
450 g shredded Monterey Jack
and Cheddar cheeses, mixed

250 ml sour cream
85 g soft white cheese, cubed
1 tablespoon chilli powder
¼ teaspoon ground cumin

1. Combine all ingredients in slow cooker.
2. Cover. Cook on high 2 hours. Stir 2 to 3 times during cooking.
3. Serve warm.

Any-Time-of-Day Cheese Dip

Prep time: 10 minutes | Cook time: 1 to 1½ hours |
Serves 12

2 (250 g) packages soft white
cheese, softened
3 (400 g) cans chilli

450 g shredded Cheddar or
Mozzarella cheese

1. Spread soft white cheese in bottom of slow cooker.
2. Spread chilli on top of soft white cheese.
3. Top with shredded cheese.
4. Cover. Cook on low 1 to 1½ hours, until shredded cheese is melted. Stir.
5. Serve.

Cheddary con Queso Dip

Prep time: 5 minutes | Cook time: 2½ to 3 hours |
Serves 8 to 10

600 g Cheddar cheese soup
or alternatively use leek and
Cheddar soup
200 g can chopped green
chillies

1 garlic clove, minced
½ teaspoon dried coriander
leaves
½ teaspoon ground cumin

1. Mix together all ingredients in slow cooker.
2. Cover. Cook on low 1 to 1½ hours. Stir well.
3. Cook an additional 1½ hours. Serve.

Hot Artichoke Dip

Prep time: 10 minutes | Cook time: 1 to 4 hours |
Makes 1.6 to 1.8 kg

2 (390 g) jars artichoke hearts
(ideally marinated), drained
375 ml fat-free mayonnaise
375 ml fat-free sour cream

225 g water chestnuts, chopped
115 g grated Parmesan cheese
115 g finely chopped spring
onions

1.Cut artichoke hearts into small pieces. Add mayonnaise, sour cream, water chestnuts, cheese, and spring onions. Pour into slow cooker.
2.Cover. Cook on high 1 to 2 hours, or on low 3 to 4 hours.
3.Serve.

Broccoli Cheese Dip

Prep time: 15 minutes | Cook time: 2 hours | Makes
1.4 kg

225 g chopped celery
115 g chopped onions
285 frozen chopped broccoli,
cooked
225 g rice, cooked

300 g fat-free, salt-free cream
of mushroom soup
1 (450 g) jar fat-free cheese
spread

1.Combine all ingredients in slow cooker.
2.Cover. Heat on low 2 hours.
3.Serve.

Hot Mushroom Dip

Prep time: 30 minutes | Cook time: 3 to 4 hours |
Serves 6 to 8

1 (250 g) package soft white
cheese
300 g cream of mushroom soup
½ (285 g) can mushrooms,

chopped and drained
160 g chopped prawn, crab, or
ham
125 ml milk

1.Cut soft white cheese into small pieces and place in slow cooker with remaining ingredients. Stir to mix.
2.Heat on low 3 to 4 hours, stirring occasionally during first hour.
3.Serve with your choice of dippers.

Soft Cheese Spread

Prep time: 5 minutes | Cook time: 2 hours | Serves
12 to 15

450 g white processed cheese,
cubed

375 ml milk

1.Combine cheese and milk in slow cooker.
2.Cover. Cook on low about 2 hours, or until cheese is melted, stirring occasionally.
3.Serve.

Crab Spread

Prep time: 20 minutes | Cook time: 4 hours | Serves 8

125 ml mayonnaise
250 g soft white cheese,
softened
2 tablespoons apple juice

1 onion, minced
450 g lump crab meat, picked
over to remove cartilage and
shell bits

1.Mix mayonnaise, cheese, and juice in medium-sized bowl until blended.
2.Stir in onions, mixing well. Gently stir in crab meat.
3.Place in slow cooker, cover, and cook on low for 4 hours.
4.Dip will hold for 2 hours. Stir occasionally. Serve

Applesauce Apple Butter

Prep time: 5 minutes | Cook time: 8 to 10 hours |
Makes 950 g

950 g unsweetened applesauce
675 g sugar or sweeten to taste
2 teaspoons cinnamon

1 teaspoon or less ground
cloves

1.Combine all ingredients in large slow cooker.
2.Cover. Cook on high 8 to 10 hours. Remove lid during last 4 hours. Stir occasionally.

Spicy Apple Butter

Prep time: 5 minutes | Cook time: 8 to 10 hours |
Makes 2 pints

1.7 litres unsweetened
applesauce
450 to 675 g sugar

2 teaspoons cinnamon
1 teaspoon ground nutmeg
¼ teaspoon allspice

1.Combine all ingredients in slow cooker.
2.Put a layer of paper towels under lid to prevent condensation from dripping into apple butter. Cook on high 8 to 10 hours. Remove lid during last hour. Stir occasionally.

Fruit Salsa

Prep time: 15 minutes | Cook time: 2 hours | Makes 900 g

1 (298 g) can mandarin oranges
½ (410 g) can unsweetened
sliced peaches, undrained
1 (230 g) can unsweetened
pineapple chunks, undrained
1 medium onion, chopped
Half a medium green pepper,
chopped

Half a medium red pepper,
chopped
Half a medium yellow pepper,
chopped
3 garlic cloves, minced
3 tablespoons cornflour
4 teaspoons vinegar

1.Combine all ingredients in slow cooker.
2.Cover. Cook on high 2 hours, stirring occasionally.
3.Serve.

Citrus Pear Butter

Prep time: 30 minutes | Cook time: 13 hours | Makes 2 pints

10 large, well-ripened pears	1 teaspoon ground cinnamon
2 tablespoons frozen orange juice concentrate	1 teaspoon ground cloves
450 g sugar	½ teaspoon ground allspice

1. Peel and quarter pears. Place in slow cooker.
2. Cover. Cook on low 12 hours. Drain thoroughly and then discard liquid.
3. Mash or purée pears. Add remaining ingredients. Mix well and return to slow cooker.
4. Cover. Cook on high 1 hour.
5. Place in hot sterile jars and seal. Process in hot water bath for 10 minutes. Allow to cool undisturbed for 24 hours.

Brown Sugar Pear Butter

Prep time: 5 minutes | Cook time: 10 to 12 hours | Makes 6 pints

1.8 kg pear sauce	1 tablespoon lemon juice
675 g brown sugar	1 tablespoon cinnamon

1. Combine all ingredients in slow cooker.
2. Cover. Cook on high 10 to 12 hours.

No-More-Bottled Barbecue Sauce

Prep time: 10 minutes | Cook time: 3 hours | Makes 450 to 565 g sauce

225 g finely chopped onions	squeezed juice is best)
60 ml oil	3 tablespoons Worcestershire sauce
1 (190 g) can tomato paste	2 tablespoons prepared mustard
125 ml water	2 teaspoons salt
75 g brown sugar	¼ teaspoon pepper
80 ml lemon juice (freshly	

1. Combine ingredients in slow cooker.
2. Cover. Cook on low 3 hours.
3. Serve.

Apple Butter with Help from the Bees

Prep time: 5 minutes | Cook time: 14 to 15 hours | Makes about 2 pints

1.75 litres unsweetened applesauce	1 teaspoon cinnamon
500 ml apple cider	½ teaspoon ground cloves
340 g honey	½ teaspoon allspice

1. Combine all ingredients in slow cooker.
2. Mix well with whisk. Cook on low 14 to 15 hours.

Slow Cooker Spaghetti or pasta sauce

Prep time: 15 minutes | Cook time: 7 hours | Serves 6 to 8

450 g minced beef	4 garlic cloves, minced
1 medium onion, chopped	2 teaspoons dried oregano
2 (400 g) cans chopped tomatoes, with juice	1 teaspoon salt
1 (190 g) can tomato paste	2 teaspoons dried basil
1 (200 g) can tomato sauce	1 tablespoon brown sugar
1 bay leaf	½ to 1 teaspoon dried thyme

1. Brown meat and onion in saucepan. Drain well. Transfer to slow cooker.
2. Add remaining ingredients.
3. Cover. Cook on low 7 hours. If the sauce seems too runny, remove lid during last hour of cooking.

Chunky Spaghetti or pasta sauce

Prep time: 20 minutes | Cook time: 3½ to 8 hours | Makes 1.4 kg

450 g minced beef, browned and drained	sauce
250 g sausages, browned and drained	1 medium onion, chopped
1 (400 g) can Italian tomatoes with basil	1 green pepper, chopped
	225 g canned sliced mushrooms
1 (400 g) can Italian tomato	125 ml dry red wine
	2 teaspoons sugar
	1 teaspoon minced garlic

1. Combine all ingredients in slow cooker.
2. Cover. Cook on high 3½ to 4 hours, or on low 7 to 8 hours.

Fresh Mushrooms, Spaghetti, and Meat Sauce

Prep time: 30 minutes | Cook time: 6 hours | Serves 6 to 8

450 g minced beef	60 g grated Parmesan or Romano cheese
1 tablespoon oil (optional)	1 (190 g) can tomato paste
250 g mushrooms, sliced	4 (200 g) cans tomato sauce
1 medium onion, chopped	1 (400 g) can chopped or chopped tomatoes
3 garlic cloves, minced	
½ teaspoon dried oregano	
½ teaspoon salt	

1. Brown minced beef in skillet or frying pan, in oil if needed. Reserve drippings and transfer meat to slow cooker.
2. Sauté mushrooms, onion, and garlic until onions are transparent. Add to slow cooker.
3. Add remaining ingredients to cooker. Mix well.
4. Cover. Cook on low 6 hours.
5. Serve.

Garden-Fresh Chilli Sauce

Prep time: 25 minutes | Cook time: 4 hours | Makes 3.8 kg

375 ml tomato juice
12 dried red (hot chilli) peppers, chopped, or enough to make 450 g-worth
3.8 kg fresh tomatoes, peeled and chopped
450 g onions, chopped
450 g red sweet peppers, chopped

1 teaspoon ground ginger
1 teaspoon ground nutmeg
1 teaspoon whole cloves
1 bay leaf
2 teaspoons ground cinnamon
2 teaspoons salt
500 ml white vinegar
1 teaspoon whole peppercorns

1. Bring tomato juice to a boil. Place dried peppers in hot juice and allow to steep and soften for 5 minutes. Cover your hands with plastic gloves. Remove stems from dried peppers, and then purée the peppers in your food processor.
2. Combine all ingredients in large slow cooker.
3. Cover. Cook on high 4 hours.
4. Remove bay leaf.
5. Freeze or can in pint jars.

Marinara Sauce

Prep time: 15 minutes | Cook time: 6 to 10 hours | Serves 12

4 (400 g) cans low-salt whole tomatoes
1 onion, finely chopped
2 carrots, pared and finely chopped

1 clove garlic, chopped
2 tablespoons vegetable oil
1 tablespoon brown sugar
½ teaspoon salt

1. Purée tomatoes in blender or food processor.
2. In a skillet or frying pan, sauté onions, carrots, and garlic in oil until tender. Do not brown.
3. Combine all ingredients in slow cooker. Stir well.
4. Cover. Cook on low 6 to 10 hours.
5. Remove cover. Stir well.
6. Cook on high uncovered for 1 hour for a thicker marinara sauce.

Chunky Cheesy Salsa Dip

Prep time: 10 minutes | Cook time: 2 hours | Serves 8

250 g fat-free soft white cheese
225 g shredded low-fat Cheddar cheese
115 g mild or medium chunky salsa

60 ml fat-free or semi-skimmed milk
1 (227 g) bag baked tortilla chips or assorted fresh vegetables

1. Cut soft white cheese into chunks.
2. Combine soft white cheese, Cheddar cheese, salsa, and milk in slow cooker.
3. Cook on low 2 hours. Stir to blend.
4. When smooth and hot, serve with baked tortilla chips or assorted fresh vegetables.

Red Pepper Cheese Dip

Prep time: 10 minutes | Cook time: 2 hours | Serves 12 to 15

2 tablespoons olive oil
4 to 6 large red peppers, cut into 1-inch squares

250 g feta cheese
Crackers or pitta bread

1. Pour oil into slow cooker. Stir in peppers.
2. Cover. Cook on low 2 hours.
3. Serve with feta cheese on crackers.

Slimmed-Down Spaghetti or pasta sauce

Prep time: 15 minutes | Cook time: 6 to 8 hours | Serves 8

2 teaspoons olive oil
1 medium onion, finely chopped
6 cloves garlic, minced
4 (400 g) can low-salt chopped tomatoes, or 1.6 kg fresh, peeled, chopped tomatoes
1 (190 g) can low-salt tomato paste

2 teaspoons dried basil
½ teaspoon dried oregano
1 teaspoon salt
½ teaspoon black pepper
1 tablespoon sugar
2 tablespoons chopped fresh parsley

1. Heat oil in a saucepan over medium heat. Add onion and garlic. Sauté until onion becomes very soft (about 10 minutes).
2. Combine all ingredients except parsley in slow cooker.
3. Cover. Cook on low 6 to 8 hours.
4. Add parsley. Cook an additional 30 minutes.
5. Serve.

Italian Vegetable Pasta Sauce

Prep time: 25 minutes | Cook time: 5 to 18 hours | Makes 2.4 kg

3 tablespoons olive oil
225 g packed chopped fresh parsley
3 ribs celery, chopped
1 medium onion, chopped
2 garlic cloves, minced
1 (2 inch) sprig fresh rosemary, or ½ teaspoon dried rosemary
2 small fresh sage leaves, or ½

teaspoon dried sage
900 g tomato sauce
907 g chopped tomatoes
1 small dried hot chilli pepper
115 g fresh mushrooms, sliced, or 225 g sliced mushrooms, drained
1½ teaspoons salt

1. Heat oil in skillet or frying pan. Add parsley, celery, onion, garlic, rosemary, and sage. Sauté until vegetables are tender. Place in slow cooker.
2. Add tomatoes, chilli pepper, mushrooms, and salt.
3. Cover. Cook on low 12 to 18 hours, or on high 5 to 6 hours.

Hearty Broccoli-Beef Dip

Prep time: 20 minutes | Cook time: 2 to 3 hours |
Serves 24

450 g minced beef
450 g processed cheese, cubed
300 g cream of mushroom soup
285 g frozen chopped broccoli,

thawed
2 tablespoons salsa, your choice
of heat

1.Brown minced beef in non-stick skillet or frying pan. Drain.
2.Combine all ingredients in slow cooker. Mix well.
3.Cover and cook on low 2 to 3 hours, or until heated through, stirring after 1 hour.
4.Serve.

Wrapped-in-Salsa Minced beef Dip

Prep time: 10 minutes | Cook time: 1 hour | Serves
10 to 12

450 g minced beef
900 g Processed cheese, cubed
1 (454 g) jar salsa, your choice

of heat
1 tablespoon Worcestershire
sauce

1.Brown beef, crumble into small pieces, and drain.
2.Combine beef, cheese, salsa, and Worcestershire sauce in slow cooker.
3.Cover. Cook on high 1 hour, stirring occasionally until cheese is fully melted.
4.Serve immediately, or turn to low for serving up to 6 hours later.

Roasted Pepper and Artichoke Spread

Prep time: 10 minutes | Cook time: 1 hour | Makes
675 g

225 g grated Parmesan cheese
125 ml mayonnaise
1 (250 g) package soft white
cheese, softened
1 garlic clove, minced

1 (390 g) can artichoke hearts,
drained and chopped finely
75 g finely chopped roasted red
peppers

1.Combine Parmesan cheese, mayonnaise, soft white cheese, and garlic in food processor. Process until smooth. Place mixture in slow cooker.
2.Add artichoke hearts and red pepper. Stir well.
3.Cover. Cook on low 1 hour. Stir again.
4.Serve.

Slow Cooker Salsa

Prep time: 20 minutes | Cook time: 2½ to 3 hours |
Makes 450 g

10 plum tomatoes, cored
2 garlic cloves
1 medium onion, cut in wedges
2 or 3 jalapeño peppers

Half a medium green pepper,
chopped
60 g coriander or parsley leaves
½ teaspoon salt

¼ teaspoon black pepper

1.Cut a small slit in two tomatoes. Insert a garlic clove in each slit. Place tomatoes and onions in slow cooker.
2.Cut stems off jalapeños. Remove seeds for a milder salsa. Place jalapeños in slow cooker. Add chopped pepper.
3.Cover. Cook on high 2½ to 3 hours. Cool.
4.In a blender, combine the tomato mixture, coriander, salt and black pepper. Process until smooth.
5.Refrigerate leftovers.

Satisfying Slow Cooker Apple Butter

Prep time: 10 minutes | Cook time: 12 to 16 hours |
Makes 6 pints

250 ml cider or apple juice
2.4 litres unsweetened
applesauce
450 to 675 g sugar

1 teaspoon vinegar
1 teaspoon cinnamon
½ teaspoon allspice

1.Boil cider until 125 ml remains.
2.Combine all ingredients in slow cooker.
3.Cover. Cook on high 12 to 16 hours, until apple butter has cooked down to half the original amount. Put in containers and freeze.

Artichoke Dip

Prep time: 10 minutes | Cook time: 1½ hours |
Serves 6 to 10

400 g non-marinated artichoke
hearts, chopped
300 g can cream of mushroom/
roasted garlic condensed soup
225 g fat-free soft white cheese,
broken into small pieces
¼ teaspoon black pepper
⅛ teaspoon crushed red pepper
flakes (optional)

Dash of salt
115 g fat-free shredded
Parmesan cheese
115 g fat-free shredded
Mozzarella cheese
115 g sliced spring onions
115 g roasted red peppers,
chopped
Fat-free vegetable spray

1.Spray inside of slow cooker with fat-free vegetable spray.
2.Combine all ingredients in slow cooker. Mix well.
3.Cook on high 1½ hours. Reduce to low and keep warm for serving.
4.Stir just before serving.

Pineapple Sauce

Prep time: 5 minutes | Cook time: 2 hours | Serves 8

1.8 litres apple juice
425 g light crushed pineapples,
undrained
350 g sultanas

½ teaspoon ground cinnamon
½ teaspoon ground allspice
115 g sugar
60 g cornflour

1.Combine all ingredients in slow cooker. Mix well.
2.Cover. Cook on high 2 hours.
3.Serve.

Revved-Up Chilli Dip

Prep time: 10 minutes | Cook time: 2 hours | Serves 15

680 g salsa
1 (435 g) can chilli with beans

65 sliced ripe olives, drained
340 g Processed cheese, cubed

1. In slow cooker, combine salsa, chilli, and olives. Stir in cheese.
2. Cover and cook on low 2 hours, or until cheese is melted, stirring halfway through.
3. Serve.

Traditional Apple Butter

Prep time: 15 minutes | Cook time: 10 to 13 hours |
Makes 1.8 kg

12 to 14 medium, tart cooking apples (about 3.6 kg chopped)
500 ml cider or apple juice

450 g sugar
1 teaspoon ground cinnamon
⅛ to ¼ teaspoon ground cloves

1. Core and chop the apples. Do not peel them. Combine apples and cider in your slow cooker.
2. Cover and cook on low 9 to 12 hours, or until apples turn mushy and then thicken.
3. Purée apples in a food mill or sieve.
4. Return puréed mixture to your slow cooker.
5. Add sugar, cinnamon, and cloves and mix together well.
6. Cover and cook on low 1 hour.

Hint-of-Anise Apple Butter

Prep time: 15 minutes | Cook time: 14 to 18 hours |
Makes 5 pints

2.75 kg Jonathan or Winesap apples
500 ml apple cider
565 g sugar

1 teaspoon star anise (optional)
2 tablespoons lemon juice
2 sticks cinnamon

1. Peel, core, and chop apples. Combine with apple cider in large slow cooker.
2. Cover. Cook on low 10 to 12 hours.
3. Stir in sugar, star anise, lemon juice, and stick cinnamon.
4. Cover. Cook on high 2 hours. Stir. Remove lid and cook on high 2 to 4 hours more, until thickened.
5. Pour into sterilized jars and seal.

Cheesy New Orleans Prawn Dip

Prep time: 20 minutes | Cook time: 1 hours | Makes
675 to 900 g

1 slice lean turkey bacon
3 medium onions, chopped
1 garlic clove, minced
4 jumbo prawns, peeled and deveined
1 medium tomato, peeled and

chopped
675 g low-fat Monterey Jack cheese, shredded
4 drops Tabasco sauce
⅛ teaspoon cayenne pepper
Dash of black pepper

1. Cook bacon until crisp. Drain on paper towel. Crumble.
2. Sauté onion and garlic in bacon drippings.
3. Drain on paper towel. Coarsely chop prawn.
4. Combine all ingredients in slow cooker.
5. Cover. Cook on low 1 hour, or until cheese melts. Thin with milk if too thick.
6. Serve.

Heated-Up Nacho Dip

Prep time: 15 minutes | Cook time: 1 hour | Serves
10 to 12

450 g minced beef
900 g Processed cheese, cubed
1 (450 g) jar salsa, your choice

of heat
1 tablespoon Worcestershire sauce

1. Brown minced beef in non-stick skillet or frying pan. Drain.
2. Place beef in slow cooker. Add all other ingredients and blend well.
3. Cover and cook on high for 1 hour. Stir occasionally until cheese is fully melted.
4. Serve immediately, or turn to low for serving up to 6 hours later.
5. Serve.

Meat and Veggie Pasta Sauce

Prep time: 10 minutes | Cook time: 7 to 8 hours |
Serves 6

250 g minced turkey
250 g minced beef
1 rib celery, chopped
2 medium carrots, chopped
1 garlic clove, minced
1 medium onion, chopped

2 (800 g) cans chopped tomatoes with juice
½ teaspoon salt
¼ teaspoon dried thyme
1 (190 g) can tomato paste
⅛ teaspoon pepper

1. Combine turkey, beef, celery, carrots, garlic, and onion in slow cooker.
2. Add remaining ingredients. Mix well.
3. Cover. Cook on low 7 to 8 hours.
4. Serve.

Honey Apple Butter

Prep time: 10 minutes | Cook time: 16 hours | Makes
6 pints

25.4 kg tart red apples (e.g. Winesap, Rome, or Macintosh)
950 ml raw honey or least-

processed honey available
115 g cinnamon sticks
1 tablespoon salt

1. Peel, core, and slice apples.
2. Combine all ingredients in large slow cooker. If apples don't fit, continue to add them as butter cooks down.
3. Cover. Cook on high 8 hours. Stir. Remove lid and let butter cook down on low 8 additional hours. Consistency should be thick and creamy.
4. Freeze, or pack into sterilized jars and seal.

Strawberry Rhubarb Sauce

Prep time: 10 minutes | Cook time: 6 to 7 hours | Serves 8

1.35 kg sliced rhubarb
180 g sugar
1 cinnamon stick (optional)

125 ml white grape juice
450 g sliced strawberries, unsweetened

1. Place rhubarb in slow cooker. Pour sugar over. Add cinnamon stick, if you wish, and grape juice. Stir well.
2. Cover and cook on low 5 to 6 hours, or until rhubarb is tender.
3. Stir in strawberries. Cook 1 hour longer.
4. Remove cinnamon stick if you've used it. Chill.

Rhubarb Sauce

Prep time: 10 minutes | Cook time: 4 to 5 hours | Serves 6

680 g rhubarb
⅛ teaspoon salt
125 ml water

125 ml sugar
Pinch of bicarbonate of soda

1. Cut rhubarb into ½-inch thick slices.
2. Combine all ingredients except bicarbonate of soda in slow cooker. Cook on low 4 to 5 hours. Stir in bicarbonate of soda.
3. Serve chilled.

Chapter 8 Snacks and Appetisers

Chilli Rellanos

Prep time: 15 minutes | Cook time: 6 to 8 hours |
Serves 8

300 ml milk
4 eggs, beaten
3 tablespoons flour

340 g chopped green chillies
450 g shredded Cheddar cheese

1. Combine all ingredients in slow cooker until well blended.
2. Cover and cook on low for 6 to 8 hours.
3. Serve.

Cheesy Tomato Pizza Fondue

Prep time: 15 minutes | Cook time: 1 hour | Serves 4 to 6

1 (450 g) block of cheese, your choice of good melting cheese, cut in ½-inch cubes
450 g shredded Mozzarella cheese
540 g Italian-style stewed

tomatoes with juice or chopped tomatoes
Loaf of Italian bread e.g. ciabatta or piadina, slices toasted and then cut into 1-inch cubes

1. Place cheese cubes, shredded Mozzarella cheese, and tomatoes in a lightly greased slow cooker.
2. Cover and cook on high 45 to 60 minutes, or until cheese is melted.
3. Stir occasionally and scrape down sides of slow cooker with rubber spatula to prevent scorching.
4. Reduce heat to low and serve. (Fondue will keep a smooth consistency for up to 4 hours.)
5. Serve with toasted bread cubes for dipping.

"Baked" Brie with Cranberry Chutney

Prep time: 10 minutes | Cook time: 4 hours | Serves 8 to 10

225 g fresh or dried cranberries
115 g brown sugar
80 ml cider vinegar
2 tablespoons water or orange juice
2 teaspoons minced crystallized ginger

¼ teaspoon cinnamon
⅛ teaspoon ground cloves
Oil
1 (225 g) round of Brie cheese
1 tablespoon sliced almonds, toasted
Crackers

1. Mix together cranberries, brown sugar, vinegar, water or juice, ginger, cinnamon, and cloves in slow cooker.
2. Cover. Cook on low 4 hours. Stir once near the end to see if it is thickening. If not, remove lid, turn heat to high and cook 30 minutes without lid.
3. Put cranberry chutney in covered container and chill for up to 2 weeks. When ready to serve, bring to room temperature.
4. Brush ovenproof plate with oil, place unpeeled Brie on plate, and bake uncovered at 350ºF (180ºC) for 9 minutes, until cheese is soft and partially melted. Remove from oven.
5. Top with at least half the chutney and garnish with almonds. Serve with crackers.

Cider Cheese Fondue—for a Buffet Table

Prep time: 15 minutes | Cook time: 4 minutes |
Serves 4

180 ml apple juice or cider
450 g shredded Cheddar cheese
225 g shredded Swiss cheese
1 tablespoon cornflour

⅛ teaspoon pepper
450 g loaf French bread, cut into chunks

1. In a large saucepan, bring cider to a boil. Reduce heat to medium low.
2. In a large mixing bowl, toss together the cheeses with cornflour and pepper.
3. Stir mixture into cider. Cook and stir for 3 to 4 minutes, or until cheese is melted.
4. Transfer to a 1 litre slow cooker to keep warm. Stir occasionally
5. Serve with bread cubes for dipping.

Party Time Artichokes

Prep time: 10 minutes | Cook time: 2½ to 4 hours |
Serves 4

4 whole, fresh artichokes
1 teaspoon salt
4 tablespoons lemon juice,

divided
2 tablespoons butter, melted

1. Wash and trim off the tough outer leaves and around the bottom of the artichokes. Cut off about 1 inch from the tops of each, and trim off the tips of the leaves. Spread the top leaves apart and use a long-handled spoon to pull out the fuzzy chokes in their centres.
2. Stand the prepared artichokes upright in the slow cooker. Sprinkle each with ¼ teaspoon salt.
3. Spoon 2 tablespoons lemon juice over the artichokes. Pour in enough water to cover the bottom half of the artichokes.
4. Cover and cook on high for 2½ to 4 hours.
5. Serve with melted butter and remaining lemon juice for dipping.

Slim Dunk

Prep time: 10 minutes | Cook time: 1 hour | Serves 12

500 ml fat-free sour cream
60 ml fat-free miracle whip
salad dressing or plain Greek
yoghurt
285 g frozen chopped spinach,

squeezed dry and chopped
50 g dry leek soup mix or if
unavailable use onion/garlic
powder
60 g red pepper, minced

1.Combine all ingredients in slow cooker. Mix well.
2.Cover. Cook on high 1 hour.
3.Serve.

Pickled Whiting

Prep time: 10 minutes | Cook time: 3 to 4 hours | Serves 24

2 onions, sliced
250 ml white vinegar
180 g Splenda
1 teaspoon salt

1 tablespoon allspice
900 g frozen individual whiting
with skin (use hake or cod if
unavailable)

1.Combine onions, vinegar, Splenda, salt, and allspice in bottom of
slow cooker.
2.Slice frozen whiting into 2-inch slices, each with skin on. Place
fish in slow cooker, pushing it down into the liquid as much as
possible.
3.Cook on low 3 to 4 hours.
4.Pour cooking liquid over fish, cover, and refrigerate. Serve when
well chilled.

Simmered Smoked Sausages

Prep time: 15 minutes | Cook time: 4 hours | Serves 16 to 20

2 (400 g) packages miniature
smoked sausages
225 g brown sugar, packed

115 g ketchup
60 g prepared horseradish

1.Place sausages in slow cooker.
2.Combine remaining ingredients in a bowl and pour over sausages.
3.Cover and cook on low for 4 hours.

Slow Cooked Smokies

Prep time: 5 minutes | Cook time: 6 to 7 hours | Serves 12 to 16

900 g miniature smoked
sausages
800 g barbecue sauce
300 ml water

3 tablespoons Worcestershire
sauce
3 tablespoons steak sauce
½ teaspoon pepper

1.In a slow cooker, combine all ingredients. Mix well.
2.Cover and cook on low 6 to 7 hours.

Tangy Cocktail Sausages

Prep time: 10 minutes | Cook time: 1 to 2 hours | Serves 12

400 g redcurrant jam
60 g prepared mustard
3 tablespoons dry sherry
¼ teaspoon ground allspice

850 g unsweetened pineapple
chunks
170 g low-salt cocktail sausages

1.Melt jam in slow cooker turned on high. Stir in seasonings until
blended.
2.Drain pineapple chunks and any liquid in cocktail sausage
package. Discard juice. Gently stir pineapple and franks into slow
cooker.
3.Cover. Cook on low 1 to 2 hours.
4.Serve and enjoy.

Sausages in Wine

Prep time: 15 minutes | Cook time: 1 hour | Serves 6

225 ml dry red wine
2 tablespoons redcurrant jam

6 to 8 mild Italian or Polish
sausages

1.Place wine and jam in slow cooker. Heat until jam is dissolved,
and sauce begins to simmer. Add sausages.
2.Cover and cook on high 45 minutes to 1 hour, or until sausages
are cooked through and lightly glazed.
3.Transfer sausages to a cutting board and slice. Serve.

Mini Hot Dogs and Meatballs

Prep time: 5 minutes | Cook time: 2 to 3 hours | Serves 15

36 frozen cooked Italian
meatballs (14 g each)
450 g package miniature hot
dogs or little smoked sausages

740 g meatless spaghetti or
pasta sauce
510 g barbecue sauce
340 g chilli sauce

1.Combine all ingredients in slow cooker.
2.Cover and cook on high 2 hours, or on low 3 hours, until heated
through.

Meaty Buffet Favourites

Prep time: 5 minutes | Cook time: 2 hours | Serves 24

225 g tomato sauce
1 teaspoon Worcestershire
sauce
½ teaspoon prepared mustard

2 tablespoons brown sugar
450 g prepared meatballs or
mini-sausages

1.Mix first four ingredients in slow cooker.
2.Add meatballs or mini-sausages
3.Cover and cook on high for 2 hours. Turn to low and serve as an
appetizer from the slow cooker.

Easy Barbecue Smokies

Prep time: 5 minutes | Cook time: 2 hours | Serves 12 to 16

500 g bottle barbecue sauce
250 g salsa
2 (400 g) packages little

smokies (miniature smoked sausages)

1. Mix barbecue sauce and salsa in slow cooker.
2. Add the little smokies.
3. Heat on high for 2 hours.
4. Stir. Turn to low to serve.

Hearty Beef Dip Fondue

Prep time: 20 minutes | Cook time: 6 hours | Makes 560 g

420 ml milk
2 (250 g) packages soft white cheese, cubed
2 teaspoons dry mustard
60 g chopped spring onions

70 g sliced dried beef, shredded or torn into small pieces
French bread, cut into bite-sized pieces, each having a side of crust

1. Heat milk in slow cooker on high.
2. Add cheese. Stir until melted.
3. Add mustard, spring onions, and dried beef. Stir well.
4. Cover. Cook on low for up to 6 hours.
5. Serve by dipping bread pieces on long forks into mixture.

Mustard-Lovers' Party Dogs

Prep time: 15 minutes | Cook time: 1 to 2 hours | Serves 12

12 hot dogs, cut into bite-size pieces
225 g grape, strawberry or

raspberry jam
225 g prepared mustard

1. Place all ingredients in slow cooker. Stir well.
2. Turn on high until mixture boils. Stir.
3. Turn to low and bring to the buffet table.

Mini Hot Dogs

Prep time: 5 minutes | Cook time: 4 to 5 hours | Serves 20 to 30 as an appetizer

450 g brown sugar
1 tablespoon Worcestershire sauce

400 g ketchup
900 g or 1.4 kg mini hot dogs

1. In slow cooker, mix together brown sugar, Worcestershire sauce, and ketchup.
2. Stir in hot dogs.
3. Cover and cook on high 1 hour. Turn to low and cook 3 to 4 hours.
4. Serve from the cooker while turned to low.

Peanut Clusters

Prep time: 20 minutes | Cook time: 3 hours | Makes 3½ to 4 dozen pieces

900 g white candy coating or white baking chocolate, chopped
340 g semi-sweet chocolate chips

1 (115 g) milk chocolate bar, or 1 (115 g) package German sweet chocolate, chopped
680 g jar dry roasted peanuts
Non-stick cooking spray

1. Spray inside of slow cooker with non-stick cooking spray.
2. In slow cooker, combine white candy coating, chocolate chips, and milk chocolate.
3. Cover and cook on low 3 hours. Stir every 15 minutes.
4. Add peanuts to melted chocolate. Mix well.
5. Drop by tablespoonfuls onto waxed paper. Cool until set. Serve immediately, or store in a tightly covered container, separating layers with waxed paper. Keep cool and dry.

Butterscotch Haystacks

Prep time: 15 minutes | Cook time: 15 minutes | Makes 3 dozen pieces

170 g butterscotch pieces
175 g chopped almonds

145 g chow mein noodles

1. Turn cooker to high. Place butterscotch pieces in slow cooker. Stir every few minutes until they're melted.
2. When the butterscotch is completely melted, gently stir in almonds and noodles.
3. When well mixed, drop by teaspoonfuls onto waxed paper.
4. Let stand until haystacks are set, or speed things up by placing them in the fridge until set.
5. Serve, or store in a covered container, placing waxed paper between layers of candy. Keep in a cool, dry place.

All American Snack

Prep time: 10 minutes | Cook time: 3 hours | Makes 3.8 kg snack mix

675 g thin pretzel sticks
900 g Wheat Chex, shredded wheat or similar
900 g Cheerios
340 g can salted peanuts
60 g butter, melted

1 teaspoon garlic powder
1 teaspoon celery salt
½ teaspoon seasoned salt
2 tablespoons grated Parmesan cheese

1. Combine pretzels, cereal, and peanuts in large bowl.
2. Melt butter. Stir in garlic powder, celery salt, seasoned salt, and Parmesan cheese. Pour over pretzels and cereal. Toss until well mixed.
3. Pour into large slow cooker. Cover. Cook on low 2½ hours, stirring every 30 minutes. Remove lid and cook another 30 minutes on low.
4. Serve warm or at room temperature. Store in tightly covered container.

Barbecued Lil' Smokies

Prep time: 5 minutes | Cook time: 4 hours | Serves 48 to 60 as an appetizer

4 (400 g) packages little smokies (miniature smoked sausages)
500 g barbecue sauce

1. Mix ingredients together in slow cooker.
2. Cover and cook on low for 4 hours.

Apple Kielbasa

Prep time: 15 minutes | Cook time: 6 to 8 hours | Serves 12

900 g fully cooked kielbasa sausage, cut into 1-inch pieces
175 g brown sugar
225 g chunky applesauce
2 cloves garlic, minced

1. Combine all ingredients in slow cooker.
2. Cover and cook on low 6 to 8 hours until thoroughly heated.

Liver Pâté

Prep time: 15 minutes | Cook time: 4 to 5 hours | Makes 340 g pâté

450 g chicken livers
225 ml dry wine
1 teaspoon instant chicken bouillon granules
1 teaspoon minced parsley
1 tablespoon instant minced onion
¼ teaspoon ground ginger
½ teaspoon seasoned salt
1 tablespoon soy sauce
¼ teaspoon dry mustard
60 g soft butter
1 tablespoon brandy

1. In slow cooker, combine all ingredients except butter and brandy.
2. Cover. Cook on low 4 to 5 hours. Let stand in liquid until cool.
3. Drain. Place in blender or food grinder. Add butter and brandy. Process until smooth.
4. Serve.

Snack Mix

Prep time: 10 minutes | Cook time: 2 hours | Serves 10 to 14

1.8 kg cereal such as shredded wheat, of any combination
1.35 kg pretzels
6 tablespoons butter, melted
2 tablespoons Worcestershire sauce
1 teaspoon seasoned salt
½ teaspoon garlic powder
½ teaspoon onion salt
½ teaspoon onion powder

1. Combine first two ingredients in slow cooker.
2. Combine butter and seasonings. Pour over dry mixture. Toss until well mixed.
3. Cover. Cook on low 2 hours, stirring every 30 minutes.

Curried Almonds

Prep time: 5 minutes | Cook time: 3 to 4½ hours | Makes 900 g nuts

2 tablespoons butter, melted
1 tablespoon curry powder
½ teaspoon seasoned salt
450 g blanched almonds

1. Combine butter with curry powder and seasoned salt.
2. Pour over almonds in slow cooker. Mix to coat well.
3. Cover. Cook on low 2 to 3 hours. Turn to high. Uncover cooker and cook 1 to 1½ hours.
4. Serve hot or cold.

Tangy Meatballs

Prep time: 15 minutes | Cook time: 2 to 4 hours | Makes 50 to 60 meatballs

900 g precooked meatballs
450 g barbecue sauce
250 g grape or redcurrant ham

1. Place meatballs in slow cooker.
2. Combine barbecue sauce and jam in medium-sized mixing bowl.
3. Pour over meatballs and stir well.
4. Cover and cook on high 2 hours, or on low 4 hours.
5. Turn to low and serve.

Sweet 'n Sour Meatballs

Prep time: 10 minutes | Cook time: 2 to 4 hours | Serves 15 to 20

340 g grape, redcurrant, raspberry or strawberry jam
340 g chilli sauce
900 g prepared frozen meatballs, thawed

1. Combine jam and sauce in slow cooker. Stir well.
2. Add meatballs. Stir to coat.
3. Cover and heat on low 4 hours, or on high 2 hours. Keep slow cooker on low while serving.

Chilli Nuts

Prep time: 5 minutes | Cook time: 2 to 2½ hours | Makes 1.1 kg nuts

60 g butter, melted
340 g cocktail peanuts
45 g chilli seasoning mix

1. Pour butter over nuts in slow cooker.
2. Sprinkle in dry chilli mix. Toss together. Cover. Heat on low 2 to 2½ hours. Turn to high. Remove lid and cook 10 to 15 minutes.
3. Serve warm or cool.

Slow Cooker Candy

Prep time: 10 minutes | Cook time: 2 hours | Makes 80 to 100 pieces

680 g white baking chocolate, broken
115 g Baker's Brand German or other sweet chocolate bar, broken
250 g chocolate chips

250 g peanut butter chips
900 g lightly salted or unsalted peanuts

1. Spray inside of cooker with non-stick cooking spray.
2. Layer ingredients into slow cooker in the order given above.
3. Cook on low 2 hours. Do not stir or lift the lid during the cooking time.
4. After 2 hours, mix well.
5. Drop by teaspoonfuls onto waxed paper. Refrigerate for approximately 45 minutes before serving or storing.

Printed in Great Britain
by Amazon

16789829R00045